Now You're Talking! ²

Strategies for Conversation

JEANNETTE D. BRAGGER

JANET SOLBERG

NATIONAL GEOGRAPHIC LEARNING | **HEINLE CENGAGE Learning**

Australia • Brazil • Japan • Korea • Mexico • Singapore • Spain • United Kingdom • United States

NATIONAL GEOGRAPHIC LEARNING | **HEINLE** CENGAGE Learning·

Now You're Talking! 2
Strategies for Conversation
Jeannette D. Bragger and Janet Solberg

Publisher: Sherrise Roehr

Executive Editor: Laura Le Dréan

Acquisitions Editor: Tom Jefferies

Development Editor: Michael Poor

Director of Global Marketing: Ian Martin

Academic Marketing Manager: Emily Stewart

Product Marketing Manager: Anders Bylund

Director of Content and Media Production:
  Michael Burggren

Senior Content Project Manager:
  Maryellen E. Killeen

Associate Content Project Manager:
  Mark Rzeszutek

Manufacturing Manager: Marcia Locke

Senior Manufacturing Buyer:

Mary Beth Hennebury

Cover Design: PreMediaGlobal

Cover Image: M.L. Campbell/Getty Images

Interior Design: PreMediaGlobal

Composition: PreMediaGlobal

Library of Congress Control Number: 2011942402

ISBN-13: 978-1-111-35057-4

ISBN-10: 1-111-35057-4

National Geographic Learning
20 Channel Center Street
Boston, MA 02210
USA

Cengage Learning is a leading provider of customized learning solutions with office locations around the globe, including Singapore, the United Kingdom, Australia, Mexico, Brazil, and Japan.

Cengage Learning products are represented in Canada by Nelson Education, Ltd.

Visit National Geographic Learning online at **elt.heinle.com**

Visit our corporate website at **www.cengage.com**

Instructors: Please visit **login.cengage.com** and log in to access instructor-specific resources.

Printed in China
2 3 4 5 6 7 16 15 14 13 12

Table of Contents

TO THE INSTRUCTOR

Introduction

Now You're Talking! is a three-level English conversation series (listening and speaking) designed for courses at the intermediate level (low-intermediate to high-intermediate). The program's particular approach to conversation is based on communicative strategies applied to a variety of contexts and topics.

This approach takes into account the varying linguistic levels of students in a typical class. The program systematically encourages them to activate their prior knowledge of vocabulary and grammatical structures in the context of face-to-face interactions based on real-life communicative situations.

Now You're Talking! consistently uses communicative strategies to help students learn and solidify high-frequency phrases, reactivate vocabulary, and add to their lexical repertoire. Students will find that their conversation skills spiral upward in more complex ways as they progress through the three-level program.

Challenges of the intermediate level and the *Now You're Talking!* solutions

Typically, the intermediate range of proficiency presents two major challenges for classroom instruction in listening and speaking.

1. Varying linguistic skills

Students arrive with a variety of abilities, skills, exposure time, and background in English. Most significantly, at each phase of learning, these students have added more and more language (vocabulary, grammar, etc.) with little time to reactivate, integrate, and solidify what they learned previously. Eventually, they are all classified as intermediate users of English and find themselves working together in the same classrooms.

The *Now You're Talking!* Solution

Now You're Talking! is designed to help "organize" the English that students already know and to do so in interactions with each other. Each chapter begins by asking students to reactivate and note previously learned English. Later in the chapter, they compare their lists of words and phrases with those of other classmates. In this way, they remind themselves of what they already know and also learn new ways of expressing themselves from other students and the instructor.

Imagine this approach as a spiral. At the bottom of the spiral, students **reactivate** previously learned material. Moving upward on the spiral, they **integrate** new information with what is known. Finally, as they move to the next segment of the spiral, they **solidify** listening and speaking skills with practice in structured and open-ended activities based on authentic real-life situations. Unlike the linear "add-on" approach used in so many other series, *Now You're Talking!* gives students time to work at their own level with regularity and to organize their communicative skills before being asked to move upward again.

2. The nature of conversation

Often in classroom settings, the short exchanges that involve single questions and answers are confused with conversations. In addition, students are often told what to say and how to say it. While such exchanges may be useful practice for newly learned grammar and vocabulary, they cannot be considered "conversing." Conversations are relatively complex segments of discourse that usually involve multiple communicative strategies. If students are limited mostly to structured and controlled activities, their ability to be involved in real-life conversations is, by extension, also limited.

Students may know some communicative strategies, but they may not necessarily have learned to combine them in unpredictable and open-ended situations. They may know a great deal of vocabulary while lacking the strategies that help them make sense of the isolated words. As a result, many students are left behind in multi-party conversations that feature authentic speech, utterances of various lengths, topic changes, hesitations, repetitions, overlapping speech, muddled enunciation, accent variations, ambient noise, and so forth.

The *Now You're Talking!* Solution

In *Now You're Talking!* students will enhance their conversational skills by

- listening to speech samples that simulate, to the extent possible, **authentic speech**. The listening strategies and activities guide students in such a way that they become quickly accustomed to the speech that they encounter in real-life situations.
- activating language systematically before they enter into conversations (**preparation**).
- focusing on the **communicative strategies** that enable them to assemble isolated words in ways appropriate to the contexts and topics. These strategies are used in a wide variety of contexts and are recycled on a regular basis.
- integrating what they have learned in controlled activities into **open-ended, less predictable conversations**. At this integrative point, the various aids and guides are withdrawn, and students must find ways to cope successfully in conversations that are very likely to occur in daily life.

Most day-to-day, non-technical conversations by native speakers are conducted at what might be termed the "intermediate" level. Therefore, students of English at the intermediate level probably already have many of the pieces needed to participate in such conversations. The challenge is to help them put the pieces together so that they can, in fact, be successful and more secure in their interactions with other speakers of English. It is this "putting together" that is the main goal of this conversation series.

Now You're Talking! Program Structure

The program has three levels.

Student Books

- Each book begins with a preliminary chapter followed by eight chapters and a speaker's handbook of communicative phrases.
- Each chapter is divided into two parts and ends with a cumulative "Improvise" section.

Schematic Chapter Outline

Part 1

Prepare: Pre-listening, Listening, Communicative Strategies, Practice Activities

Talk: Speaking Activities (pairs, small groups, whole class)

Part 2

Prepare: Listening Comprehension (Listening Strategy), Communicative Strategies, Practice Activities

Talk: Speaking Activities (whole class, pairs, small groups)

Improvise

Cumulative listening and speaking activities, Internet activity

- Each chapter also contains three "floating" features that spin off from the chapter content and appear where logically useful to students:

Language Focus: Highlights a grammatical structure or a lexical issue.

Professional Context: Highlights the communicative strategies or linguistic behaviors appropriate in professional settings (business, academia).

Cultural Connections: Highlights cultural topics about the United States as they relate to the chapter's communicative strategies. Students are asked to make comparisons with their own cultures.

- Each chapter contains a variety of activity types, from controlled practice to semi-controlled practice to open-ended activities. As deemed necessary, activities are supported by models.
- Chapter content is supported by art, photos, and realia.

Audio Program

- Each Student Book has a corresponding Student CD containing the audio materials. Complete audio scripts appear in the Student Book after Chapter 8.
- Audio recordings strive for authentic, natural speech.

Instructor's Guide

An Instructor's Guide for each level includes

- chapter summaries (content, grammar, vocabulary, communicative strategies)
- activity management (small group, whole class, etc.)
- suggestions for brainstorming activities
- suggestions for follow-up activities
- activity cards
- answers keys
- testing and evaluation techniques

Summary

Books 1 through 3 of *Now You're Talking!* generally progress as indicated in the chart below. Recycling, repetition, and spiraling upward of both speaking/listening strategies and topics are integral to the series.

Book 1		Book 3
low-intermediate to intermediate	→	intermediate to high-intermediate
communicative strategies to topics	→	topics to communicative strategies
immediate environment	→	turning outward, toward the world
familiar	→	less familiar, but not unknown
sentences / multiple sentences (shorter discourse)	→	multiple sentences / paragraphs (longer discourse)
concrete	→	concrete / abstract
high-frequency	→	high- to lower-frequency

TO THE STUDENT

Now You're Talking! teaches you how to participate actively in conversations. You already know a lot of vocabulary. Now you'll learn the communicative strategies that help you put the words together. Communicative strategies are phrases that you need to participate appropriately in conversations. You'll learn phrases to ask for and give an opinion; phrases to ask for clarification or for more information; phrases to show your emotions; and many more. Communicative strategies help all speakers of English to communicate in real life, in real situations, with real people.

Conversation is like a ball game. A good player knows how to get the ball rolling (start a conversation), how to catch the ball (react), how and in which direction to throw the ball back (keep the conversation going), how to keep the ball in bounds (stay on topic), and how to guess other players' moves (be prepared for what others say). These strategies for how to play are as important as having the right ball and the right equipment.

Maybe you think that you don't know enough vocabulary to participate in a conversation or that your grammar is not good enough. Don't let that stop you from playing the conversation game. You probably know much more vocabulary and grammar than you realize. What you really need to learn are the **communicative strategies** to help you become a full conversational partner.

Each chapter in *Now You're Talking!* is divided into two parts. Each part starts with a **Prepare** section where you can learn communicative strategies in real conversations and practice them in activities. You "prepare" as assigned homework or in class before you're asked to interact with your classmates and your instructor. Then, you move to the **Talk** section. Here, you apply what you learned and have conversations with your classmates in pairs, small groups, or as a whole class. When you're done with the two parts, you'll do the final **Improvise** activities with your classmates. This section puts everything in the chapter together. You combine and review what you've learned, participating in conversations that you're likely to have in real life.

Most importantly, as you interact with your classmates and your instructor, be creative and have fun. Before long, you'll realize that *Now You're Talking!*

ACKNOWLEDGMENTS

I would like to thank John McHugh, who first approached me about writing an English conversation series. His initial enthusiasm was the encouragement I needed to enter into this project. My thanks also go to Sherrise Roehr and Thomas Jefferies, whose many accommodations were invaluable for the successful publication of *Now You're Talking!*

But most importantly, I reserve my profoundest gratitude for my editor, Michael Poor. His calm and patient approach to problems, his sense of humor, his willingness to ask questions in order to understand, his intelligence and willingness to argue, and his ability to navigate among sometimes conflicting points of view made him one of the very best editors I've worked with over the last 35 years. *Now You're Talking!* would not have seen the light of day if it had not been for Mike.

My thanks also to the following educators who provided invaluable feedback throughout the development of *Now You're Talking!*

Reviewers

Michael Chrzanowski
Community College of Denver

Jerry R. Kottom
Community College of Denver

April M. Darnell
University of Dayton IEP

Sheryl Meyer
English Language Center, University of Denver

Nancy Hamadou
Pima Community College

Anouchka Rachelson
Miami Dade College

Gail Kellersberger
University of Houston-Downtown

Scott C. Welsh
Arizona State University

DEDICATION

I dedicate *Now You're Talking!* to my friend and co-author, Donald Rice, who passed away in March 2010. He was excited about the prospect of writing this series. I think he would have been happy with the result.

Jeannette D. Bragger

Jeannette Bragger

PRELIMINARY CHAPTER
Getting Acquainted
"Nice to meet you!"

Strategies for Communication

Part 1: How to Get Acquainted

Part 2: How to Engage in Conversations

 PREPARE ◐◑

INTRODUCTION: *What Is a Conversation?*

- A conversation is a verbal exchange that involves at least two people.
- It includes vocabulary, communicative strategies, grammar, an awareness of social contexts, and other aspects of language.

A. PRE-LISTENING **What's going on?** Check what you think is happening in each series of statements: an introduction, a reaction, or the sharing of information.

	Introduction	Reaction	Information
1. Hey, Jennifer. Meet my old friend from high school. Philip, Jennifer. Jennifer, Philip.	_____	_____	_____
2. How could you possibly forget about the meeting? You're impossible!	_____	_____	_____
3. This is my assistant Michael Franklin. Michael, this is Dr. Earnhard.	_____	_____	_____
4. My parents arrived in this country from Korea in 1976.	_____	_____	_____
5. I'm moving to Connecticut in April. I'll send you my new address and phone number.	_____	_____	_____
6. Wow! I'm really happy for you. Congratulations!	_____	_____	_____
7. As far as I know, the concert starts at eight. It should be over by ten.	_____	_____	_____
8. Are you serious? Did he really say that? That's not very nice!	_____	_____	_____
9. Hi. My name is Jane Canfield.	_____	_____	_____
10. I'm really sorry you can't come to Florida with us. It would have been fun.	_____	_____	_____

B. LISTENING What did you say? Put a check (✓) in the box under the communicative strategies you hear in each conversation.

	INTRODUCTION	CLARIFICATION	GREETING	REACTION	EXCHANGE OF INFORMATION
Conversation 1					
Conversation 2					
Conversation 3					

CD 1
Track 5

C. LISTENING Getting acquainted. Listen to the conversation, and write down five things that Daniel finds out about Ivan.

1. _____
2. _____
3. _____
4. _____
5. _____

D. Conversational topics. What topics of conversation can you bring up when you're meeting a classmate for the first time? Write down five topics that are appropriate and five topics that are inappropriate.

	APPROPRIATE TOPICS	INAPPROPRIATE TOPICS
1.		
2.		
3.		
4.		
5.		

Cultural Connections: Privacy in the United States

Most cultures have very specific ideas about what the concept "privacy" means. Generally speaking, privacy refers to the parts of our lives that are closed to other people.

In the United States, people are especially private about personal information. Most do not want outsiders to know certain information, such as their age, their salary, or their political preferences. Usually people do not choose to reveal that kind of information about themselves.

On the other hand, Americans are not as private about their personal space. In contrast to many other cultures, Americans are usually happy to invite friends and acquaintances into their homes, show them around, and offer them food and drinks. The concept of privacy is different for each individual and culture. It's important to remember to respect people's privacy when you are first getting to know them.

How is privacy defined where you're from? How often are people invited into your circle of family and friends or into your home? What questions shouldn't you ask strangers or people you just met?

COMMUNICATIVE STRATEGIES: *How to Get Acquainted*

Hi, I'm Karen.

Nice to meet you, Karen. **I'm** Sam.

What do you do, Sam?

I'm a student in microbiology. **What about you?**

I play keyboard in a band.

Cool!

PHRASES

Greetings	Asking for Information	Repetition
Hi!	Who? / Whose? / Which? /	Could you repeat that?
Hello.	What? / Why (How come)? /	Sorry. What did you say?
Hey + *name*	Where? / When? / How?	**Reaction**
Introductions	**Clarification**	Really?
John, this is Carol. Carol, John.	What happened?	No kidding!
Let me introduce …	What do you mean?	Congratulations!
My name is … / I'm …	For example?	That's true.

Note: See the *Speaker's Handbook* on page 157 for additional phrases.

Yes / No **Questions with Rising Intonation**
auxiliary verb + **subject** + *verb*
Are you taking an English class this semester?
Will we have a test next week?
Do I need to bring my computer to the meeting?

Information Questions with Falling Intonation
Who's your English professor?
Whose computer are you using?
Which book are we supposed to read?
What kind of work do you do?
Why did you decide to get into psychology?
Where do you work?
When do you want to get together?
How long have you lived here?

E. **What do you want to know?** Write down six questions you could ask someone you've just met. Keep in mind what's appropriate and what's inappropriate to ask.

1. _____
   _____
   _____

2. _____
   _____
   _____

3. _____
   _____
   _____

4. _____
   _____
   _____

5. _____
   _____
   _____

6. _____
   _____
   _____

F. **Peer correction.** Discuss the topics you wrote down in Activity D with your classmates. Talk about why each topic is appropriate or inappropriate in your first conversation with someone you meet.

G. **Hi. I'm …** Move around the room, and get to know several classmates. Greet each person, introduce yourself, and then ask appropriate questions to find out some basic information about the person.

H. **Do you like music?** Introduce yourself to a classmate you've never met before. Use the **Communicative Strategies** you learned and the question forms you reviewed to find out as much as possible about each other. Ask for clarification or additional information when necessary.

Part Two

●● PREPARE ●●

LISTENING COMPREHENSION: *Identifying Subtopics in a Conversation*

When you're talking to someone you don't know well, you usually ask him or her questions about general topics. The person's response might include detailed subtopics that provide more specific information about the main topic. You need to identify subtopics in order to keep the conversation going.

- **Anticipated responses.** One way to identify the subtopics of a general topic is to anticipate possible responses. For example:

  Q: *What kind of music do you like?* (Anticipate the person will respond with specific types of music, like electronica or salsa.)

  A: *I really like salsa.*

- **Follow-up questions.** Another way to identify subtopics is to ask for clarification about a specific response. For example:

  Q: *What kind of work do you do?*

  A: *I'm a director of human resources.* (You're not sure what is meant by "human resources" and need clarification.)

  Q: *I'm not familiar with that. What do you do in human resources?*

  A: *I help the employees of our company.*

CD 1 🔊 **I.** LISTENING Subtopics. Write the three subtopics you hear in the responses to the
Tracks general questions that are asked in each conversation.
6-9

1. _____ _____ _____

2. _____ _____ _____

3. _____ _____ _____

4. _____ _____ _____

CD 1 🔊 **J.** LISTENING Choices. Listen to three conversations. For each, identify the main topic
Tracks and the subtopics.
10-12

	MAIN TOPIC	SUBTOPICS
1.		
2.		
3.		

Chris: **I totally disagree with you**. He'll never win the election!

Shel: I don't see why not. **In my opinion**, he's the best candidate.

Tamika: Why do you always have to talk about politics? It's so **boring**.

Will: I'd rather get everybody's opinions about the movies that are playing right now. I'd like to see something good tomorrow night with my girlfriend.

Darla: Well, **I think you should** absolutely go see *The King's Speech*.

PHRASES

Asking for Help

Could you help me with …?

Would you have the time to …?

Advice

What should I do?

If I were you, I would …

Description

He's tall / short / etc.

She has short hair / brown eyes / etc.

He's crazy about …

She's not into …

He's older than …

Opinion

What do you think (about) …?

In my opinion …

Agreement / Disagreement

Good idea!

I agree with …

That's true.

I disagree with you.

I don't think so.

Summarizing Questions

Who? / When? / Where? / Why? / What? / How? / What happened?

Note: See the *Speaker's Handbook* on page 157 for additional phrases.

Language Focus: Responding to Unfamiliar Words

When you participate in conversations or listen to presentations in English, you will likely hear words you don't understand. When you hear unfamiliar words, you can try to guess their meaning or ask the speaker to clarify the meaning.

From a naturalist's lecture

*We're actively involved in protecting turtles like Diamondback Terrapins. We follow the tracks of the females to the places where they lay their eggs. When the female has buried the eggs in the sand, she leaves. That's when we put wire cages around the nest to protect the eggs from **predation** by animals like coyotes, skunks, and raccoons. By protecting the eggs, we're making sure that more turtles are born.*

Guessing the meaning of *predation*

If you know the word *predator*, you might be able to guess that **predation** is what predators like coyotes, skunks, and raccoons do—one animal kills another animal for food.

Phrases to request clarification of the word *predation*

- *I'm not familiar with the word* predation.
- *I've never heard the word* predation. *What does it mean?*
- *What does* predation *mean exactly?*
- *What do you mean by* predation?
- *What is meant by* predation?
- *Can you explain the word* predation?

K. Summer plans. Imagine that summer vacation is coming. Make a list of things that someone who has no plans could do to pass the time this summer. In addition, write two phrases to express your opinion and give advice.

L. **I need some help.** What are some things that you often need help doing? Make a list of tasks that you would ask people to help you do. In addition, write two phrases that you might use to ask for help.

M. **What's the problem?** Think of a problem that a person might ask advice for. Write notes about the general and specific issues in such a problem. In addition, write two phrases you might use to summarize the problem.

👁👁 TALK 👁👁

👥 N. Summer fun! Share your list of ideas from Activity K with your classmates. Talk about various things that you could do to make your summer more interesting. Discuss the general ideas and also some subtopics.

Example: **A:** *I'm going to be so bored this summer. I have no idea what to do.*
B: *Well, what are you interested in?*
A: *I can't think of anything.*
C: *Oh, come on! I happen to know that you like to cook.*
D: *Maybe you could work in your parents' restaurant.*
A: *That's an idea. I love to cook, but I have a lot to learn.*

👥 O. Can you help me? Move around the room and ask different classmates to help you do some of the tasks you listed in Activity L. Explain what you need, and use phrases to ask for help. Your classmates will either say no and explain why not or agree to help you. React appropriately to their responses.

Example: **A:** *Hey, Enrique. Would you have time to help me create some graphics on my computer? It's for an assignment for one of my classes.*
B: *Sure, no problem. When do you want to meet?*
OR
C: *I'd like to, but it depends on how soon you need my help. I'm really busy for the next couple of days because I have an exam.*
OR
D: *I'd like to help, but I don't know anything about doing graphics. Why don't you ask Cecilia? I think she's good at graphics.*

👥 P. Here's the problem. Present the problem you outlined in Activity M to one of your classmates. Use the phrases you wrote down to summarize the problem. Then, ask your partner what you should do, and he or she will give you advice. When you're done, reverse roles.

Professional Context: Appropriate Tone in Conversations

In business and academic settings, the tone—or speaking style—of conversations is usually more formal than what you're used to with your family and friends. In most professional contexts, you are expected to:

- have a polite tone.
- not raise your voice in anger or irritation.
- use phrases like *Excuse me* or *Pardon me* when you interrupt someone.
- use the most polite forms to ask for information, clarification, advice, opinions, and repetition.

It's also important not to state your opinions or disagreements too strongly.

🞔🞔 IMPROVISE 🞔🞔

CD 1 🔊
Track
13

Q. LISTENING **Do you have a minute?** Listen to the conversation between Aksana and Eric, two colleagues in the English department. Then, answer the questions.

1. Where do you think this conversation takes place?

2. What's the first question Aksana asks Eric?

3. What's Eric's advice to her?

4. What's the second problem Aksana asks about?

5. What are the two solutions Eric proposes?

6. What does Aksana ask Eric about how students turn in their papers?

7. What's his answer?

8. What's Aksana's last question and Eric's answer?

R. **What should I do if …?** Imagine that you need advice about life on campus. Ask your classmates for advice and help.

> **Topics:**
>
> buying books / writing papers if you don't have a computer / getting help in your courses / planning your schedule for next semester / participating in social events

S. **I saw an interesting movie.** Tell your classmates about a movie you saw recently. Summarize the story (who, when, where, why, what, what happened), and then tell them why you liked or didn't like the movie.

T. **Agree or disagree.** Have short conversations with your classmates about one or more of the topics below. First, agree or disagree with the statement. Then, give your opinion about the topic. Remember to ask your classmates for their opinions.

1. Social networking sites are an invasion of privacy.

2. One of the best ways to succeed in business is to speak several languages.

3. Recycling is a waste of time. It's too late to save the environment.

4. It takes a long time to become friends with a person.

5. One of the best ways to learn is to read a lot.

U. **Nice party.** You meet a person at a party at a friend's house. Role-play the situation with a classmate by following the steps for getting acquainted.

1. Greet and introduce yourselves to each other. Make a comment about the party.

2. Ask questions about each other. Be careful not to ask inappropriate questions.

3. Figure out something that you have in common, such as a hobby or a sport. Then, share opinions about subtopics of that common interest. Use phrases to agree or disagree with the opinions.

4. Make plans to meet again (when, where, for what reason).

5. Say goodbye.

1 Talking about Places

"How do you like living here?"

Strategies for Communication

Part 1: How to Describe a Place

Part 2: How to Compare and Contrast

●● PREPARE ●●

A. PRE-LISTENING Pros and cons. Read the dialogue in which a place is described. Draw a circle ○ around the positive characteristics, and <u>underline</u> the negative characteristics.

Julius: Now that you've moved to Oregon, how do you like it?

Sven: I love it. We bought a very comfortable house on a beautiful lake and not too far from a popular ski area. The property is large with a lot of great walking trails nearby.

Julius: Is it difficult to live so far out in the country?

Sven: Well, there are some things I'm still not used to. We're pretty far from everything. The nearest hospital is an hour away. We get a lot of snow in the winter, and we have to travel far to get our groceries or go to a restaurant. And I miss my friends.

Julius: That sounds kind of lonely.

Sven: Sometimes it is. But I like everything else. The view of the mountains is amazing. The house is cozy and easy to take care of; we have a big garden where we grow vegetables and fruit, and we even have chickens. So we have fresh eggs every day. Unfortunately, a fox killed one of our chickens a week ago. That's one of the problems with living in the country. But it also makes it interesting.

Julius: I think I would have a hard time living in such an isolated place.

Sven: The setting may be a bit remote, but the house has all the modern conveniences. It's the perfect size for the two of us.

Julius: Well, it sounds like you're enjoying your new life. I'm very happy for you.

CD 1 Tracks 14-15

B. LISTENING What's your place like? Listen to the two conversations in which people talk about the places where they live. For each conversation, write down the words or phrases you hear that describe each place.

Conversation 1

_____

_____

_____

Conversation 2

_____

_____

_____

_____

CD 1
Track
16

C. LISTENING **On the first floor …** Listen to a real estate agent describe a house. Write down the words and phrases you hear that tell you how the house is arranged and where the rooms are located.

_____
_____
_____
_____
_____
_____
_____
_____
_____
_____

COMMUNICATIVE STRATEGIES: *How to Describe a Place*

Carol: I love New England in the fall. My family and I always go camping there in October.
Enrique: What's so good about it?
Carol: It's **beautiful!** The leaves are changing to their fall colors: red, brown, orange, gold. The trees are **spectacular**. We go to a **small** campground **near** a lake. There are lots of hiking trails, and sometimes it's still warm enough to go swimming.

PHRASES

Descriptions

It's (It is) / They're (They are) + adjective

Positive Adjectives

amazing	great	modern	rural
awesome	hilly	mountainous	small
beautiful	huge	peaceful	spectacular
clean	interesting	picturesque	sunny
fabulous	large	quiet	wonderful

Negative Adjectives

boring	depressing	inaccessible	polluted
busy	dirty	inconvenient	run down
crowded	expensive	isolated	small
dangerous	flat	large	stressful
dark	huge	noisy	ugly

Descriptions of Location

It's (It is) / They're (They are) + location + a place

Phrases of location

across the street from	next to	east of
behind	around the corner from	north of
in front of	not far from	south of
near	right next door to	west of

Other ways to describe places

[the house] It is white with brown trim.

[the streets] They are very narrow.

[the village] It's in a valley / on a lake / on a mountain / near the ocean.

It has / There is / There are + nouns

[the town] It has good schools. There are many restaurants and movie theaters.

[the house] It has three bedrooms. There's a lot of closet space. It has a modern kitchen.

[the house] It has a view of the ocean. / There's a water view.

Note: See the *Speaker's Handbook* on page 157 for additional phrases.

D. Describing places. Look at the places in the photos. Describe what you see in each photo and what you imagine each place to be like.

1.

_____
_____
_____
_____
_____
_____

2.

_____
_____
_____
_____
_____
_____

3.

_____
_____
_____
_____
_____
_____

4.

_____
_____
_____
_____
_____
_____

Language Focus: The Passive Voice

In sentences stated in the **active voice**, the subject *does* the action.

> **The Spanish settled** California.

In sentences stated in the **passive voice**, the subject *receives* the action.

> California **was settled** by **the Spanish**.

In the passive voice, the object (California) becomes the subject (passive role) and the subject (the Spanish) becomes the object.

Verbs in the passive voice have the form **to be + past participle**.

> The Eiffel Tower **was built** in 1889.

Verbs commonly used in the passive voice to express the past (*was / were* + verb) as related to places:

built	established	occupied	redone
closed	excavated	opened	remodeled
completed	fixed (up)	paid for	removed
constructed	founded	painted	renovated
created	inhabited	planted	repaired
designed	located	proposed	settled
destroyed	made	put in	shut down
discovered	named after	rebuilt	torn down

E. **Active or passive?** Put an **A** next to the sentences that are in the active voice and a **P** next to the ones that are in the passive voice.

1. _____ New York's Central Park was constructed in 1857.

2. _____ The French sculptor Frederic-Auguste Bartholdi created the Statue of Liberty.

3. _____ The Spanish established the city of San Francisco in 1776.

4. _____ The Golden Gate Bridge in San Francisco was opened to traffic on May 28, 1937.

5. _____ The city of Houston was named after General Sam Houston, hero of the War of 1812.

6. _____ The National Museum of American History in Washington was renovated between 2006 and 2008.

7. _____ Hiram Bingham discovered the ruins of Machu Picchu in 1911.

8. _____ The Vietnam Veterans Memorial Wall in Washington, D.C., was designed by U.S. architect Maya Lin.

F. The place where you live. Make a list of words and phrases that describe the place where you live (your region, state, town). If you know the history of your area, write down some facts using the passive voice.

●● TALK ●●

G. Describing places. With your classmates, combine the descriptive words you came up with for the images in Activity D. Talk about the places based on what you actually see in the photos and also on what you imagine the places to be like.

Cultural Connections: Use of Living Space

Different cultures vary in the way they organize and use their living space. The factors that determine what one's living space is like include social standing, religion, traditions, lifestyle, comfort, privacy, natural surroundings, climate, and the availability of space.

For example, because the climate in much of the United States is mild, many houses have outdoor lawns for play and entertainment. But in places like Morocco where the climate is very hot, some houses are built around large open courtyards where people can gather and stay cool.

Another cultural difference is in how people use their living space. For example, in most Western cultures, families and friends eat meals while sitting on chairs around a table, usually in a dining room. In other cultures, people may have their meals while sitting on cushions on the floor, or outside around a fire.

The way that people organize and use their living space can tell you a great deal about their lives, their environment, and what they value.

What are the characteristics of typical houses where you're from? What factors influence the way they're organized and used?

Entertainment area in an American beach house

Interior courtyard for entertaining in a Moroccan home

H. **The place where we live.** Have a conversation with your classmates about the place where you live (your region, state, town). Your descriptions should include the words and phrases from your lists in Activity F. You may not always agree with each other. If not, give reasons for your opinions.

I. **If I had to choose …** With a classmate, talk about the real estate ads for houses using the descriptions and the photos. After you've talked about each house, decide which one you prefer and explain why.

1.

Located in a quiet neighborhood, this home was completely renovated in 2005. The first floor has a large family room, an eat-in kitchen with granite countertops, and a master bedroom with private bath. The second floor has 3 bedrooms with 1 full bath.

2.

This ranch-style home has a lake view. The house has a new roof and new windows. The single-level floor plan includes 3 bedrooms, 2 full baths, a spacious living room, a laundry room, and a recently renovated kitchen. A one-car garage was added last year.

3.

This new construction in a secluded setting is scheduled to be completed in the fall. It has a master suite with a fireplace, 4 additional bedrooms, 3 full baths, a large kitchen next to a dining room, and a large landscaped backyard with a brick patio. The wide porch is ideal for entertaining.

4.

Beautifully restored apartment with 3 bedrooms, an office with built-in bookcases, a family room with a brick fireplace, and 2½ baths. Hardwood floors throughout. Roof deck offers a full view of the river.

Part Two

●● PREPARE ●●

LISTENING COMPREHENSION: *Listening for Details: Understanding Location Words*

When you listen to someone describe a place, pay attention to the words and phrases that help you understand location.

- Words like **east, west, south, north, upstairs, downstairs, next to, in front of,** and **far from** are location words that help you figure out where something is in relation to other places.
- Many prepositions are also important for understanding where something is located. Listen for prepositions such as **above, around, before, below, down, in, near, on, over, toward, under,** and **up** to get a clearer mental picture of what places might look like.
- Be careful, however, because some prepositions have other meanings besides their use as location words. Here are some examples.

    Go **up** to your room. / Clean **up** that mess.
    My house is **around** the block. / I'll be **around**.
    Stop **before** you get to the light. / You've never been here **before**?

CD 1 Track 17 **J.** **LISTENING An American home.** Answer the questions about the house plan based on what you hear in the conversation.

1. How many floors does the house have? _____

2. Where is the living room in relation to the kitchen? _____

3. Where is the deck? _____

4. Where is the laundry room? _____

5. Where is the first-floor bathroom? _____

6. How do you get to the second floor? _____

7. Where are the two small bedrooms? _____

8. What else is on the second floor and where? _____

9. Where are the storage spaces? _____

10. What kind of neighborhood is the house in? _____

CD 1 Track 18 **K.** **How do I get there?** Listen to the conversation for the directions on how to get to the Georgia Aquarium in Atlanta. As you listen, complete the steps of the directions.

Starting Point: Marietta, Ga.
Destination: Georgia Aquarium
225 Baker Street Northwest
Atlanta, Ga.

1. Head _____ on _____ Park Square _____ Whitlock Avenue Northwest.

2. Take the _____ onto South Park Square Southeast.

3. _____ onto Roswell Street for _____ a mile.

4. Turn _____ onto Cobb Parkway Southeast.

5. _____ onto South Marietta Parkway Southeast.

6. _____ the ramp onto 1-75 South.

7. Take exit _____ toward the aquarium.

8. _____ onto Ivan Allen Junior Boulevard.

9. Turn _____ onto Centennial Olympic Park Drive Northwest.

10. Take the _____ onto Baker Street Northwest. The aquarium is _____.

COMMUNICATIVE STRATEGIES: *How to Compare and Contrast*

Tracy: I prefer living in the country. It's peaceful, it's clean, there's not a lot of crime …

Cedric: Well, it's true that small towns are **quieter** and **less polluted than** the city, **but** it's **more fun** to live in the city.

PHRASES

Comparing (Similarities)	Contrasting (Differences)
similar (to)	different (than)
the same (as)	the opposite (of)
alike	not the same (at all)
also	however
too	but
both	on the other hand
not only … but also	except
neither	while
(just) as + *adjective* + as + *noun*	(much) more / less + *adjective* + than …
doesn't / don't + (*verb* +) either …	-er *form of adjectives* (e.g., noisi**er**)
I don't like country living. My husband to *Boise doesn't have a subway. Nampa*	Cities are **more congested** and **noisier** than small towns. (*The two are different.*)

Note: See the *Speaker's Handbook* on page 157 for additional phrases.

L. Similarities and differences. Fill in the blanks using expressions from the **Communicative Strategies** that best complete the sentences.

1. The two apartments we looked at are very _____. The first one is _____ than the second one. It has three bedrooms, _____ the second one has only two.

2. The two houses are _____ in a couple ways. First, _____ of them are far from my office. Second, _____ are they small, _____ they're a little run-down.

3. My sister and I are very _____. She loves going to the movies, and I do _____. I don't like seafood, and _____ does she.

4. My dorm room is exactly _____ as every other dorm room on campus. It's _____ small as the others and it has _____ furniture. _____, after they're decorated, the rooms are not _____. For example, my room is _____ colorful than Alice's. And my room is usually _____ than Alice's, because hers is usually messy.

5. My parents are very active. They _____ like to play golf together, _____ they love camping and hiking. They're similar in every way _____ when it comes to their opinions about baseball. Mom likes the New York Yankees, _____ Dad is a Boston Red Sox fan.

Language Focus: *Comparatives and Superlatives of* Good *and* Bad

Good: not as good as, as good as, better than, the best
Bad: not as bad as, as bad as, worse than, the worst

M. Academic performance. The chart compares the academic performance of four students. Use the information to make at least six comparisons between them. You'll make more comparisons when you discuss the students with your classmates.

Examples: Jorge is busier than the other students because he's taking more classes than the others.
Naoki got a much better score on the English exam than Jorge.

NAME	NUMBER OF CLASSES THIS SEMESTER	SCORE ON ENGLISH PLACEMENT EXAM	GRADE IN BIOLOGY	GRADE IN HISTORY	OVERALL GRADE POINT AVERAGE
Jorge (m.)	6	62%	B+	D	2.4
Maya (f.)	4	85%	A-	B	3.2
Soon-yi (f.)	5	78%	A	C	2.9
Naoki (m.)	3	91%	B	A+	3.7

1. _____

2. _____

3. _____

4. _____

5. _____

6. _____

N. **Country or city?** Make a list of the advantages and disadvantages of living in the country and the city. You'll discuss your thoughts with a classmate.

	Living in the Country	Living in the City
Advantages		
Disadvantages		

Professional Context: Office Space

As with living space, culture and environment also determine how professional office space is organized. In the United States, for example, some companies want to make sure the work space allows workers to be very productive, while other companies try to make their space more pleasant and carefree. Nearly all offices have break rooms, refrigerators, microwaves, and vending machines. Other offices offer more perks like childcare services and exercise equipment.

Company executives usually have the biggest offices. People compete for the "corner office," one that has windows on two walls and a nice view. Executive offices are often clearly separated from lower-level employees and may be located on higher floors of the building. Generally in corporate America, the bigger your office, the higher your status.

●● TALK ●●

O. **Academic performance.** Talk to your classmates about the comparisons you made in Activity M and make sure they're true. Then, continue the conversation about the four students, adding as many comparisons as you can think of.

Use these questions to help you get started:

1. Who probably studies the hardest?
2. Who has a better command of English?
3. Who is worse in biology than in history?
4. Who has the lowest grade point average?
5. Who seems to be the best student?
6. Who seems to be the poorest student? Why?

P. Country or city? Use your list from Activity N and talk to a classmate about the advantages and disadvantages of living in the country and in the city. If you disagree with any of your classmate's comparisons, share your own opinions and give reasons to support them.

Q. Places in paintings. Talk about each painting with your classmates.

1. Say whether or not you like each painting and why.

2. Make a group description of the place depicted in the painting.

3. Compare and contrast the paintings.

Claude Monet (France), *The Poppy Field, near Argenteuil* (1873)

Francis Farmar, *Main Street: Sag Harbour, Long Island, 2006* (2006)

Ando Hiroshige (Japan), *Cherry Blossoms* (1800s)

Winslow Homer, *The Country School* (1871)

● ● IMPROVISE ● ●

CD 1 🔊 **R.** **LISTENING A visit to Paris.** Listen to Olivia tell her friend Robert about her trip to
Track   Paris. As you listen, answer the following questions. Then, compare your answers with
19   those of a classmate.

Eiffel Tower, Paris

1. What are some of the general words and phrases she uses to describe Paris?

2. What specific information does she give about the city?

3. What does she say about the hotel where she stayed?

4. How does she compare Paris to her home city of San Francisco?

S. **A place I know.** Have a conversation with a classmate about a place where you've
lived or that you've visited. Give a detailed description of the place, using descriptive
words and phrases you've learned. Also describe the weather and what you can see and
do there. Your partner can ask you questions for clarification or additional information.

T. **My dream house.** Think about what your dream house would be like. Describe your
house to a classmate. Consider these questions to help you with your description.

- Where is your dream house located?
- What are the surroundings like?
- What's the climate?
- What does it look like on the inside? (number of rooms, other features)
- What else is on the property? (pool, gardens, other features)

INTERNET RESEARCH Wonders of the world. Go online and find a description
of one of the Seven Wonders of the World (either ancient or modern). Write down the
most interesting facts you discovered, and talk to your classmates about the "wonder"
you researched.

2 Managing a Discussion

"As I was saying …"

Strategies for Communication

Part 1: How to Raise a Discussion Topic

Part 2: How to Manage a Discussion

 PREPARE ●●

A. **PRE-LISTENING You're late!** Read the conversation about the importance of being on time. Then, write down the expressions the friends use to introduce a topic in each situation.

Paul: *(running up, out of breath)* Julia! What time is it? I hope I'm not late!

Julia: No, you're fine. I was actually a few minutes early. But hey, speaking of being on time, I'd like your opinion about something that bothers me. You notice how every time the five of us go somewhere, Kelley, John, and Carlos are all late? You think I should bring this up?

Paul: I feel the same way, now that you mention it. Yeah, I think you should talk to them. *(Kelley and John arrive 20 minutes later.)*

Kelley: Hi guys! Wait till you hear what we saw on the way over! There was this guy in a cowboy costume, right, and …

Julia: You should tell us all about it on the way to the restaurant. But first, um …, this isn't easy, but we wanted to talk to you guys about being more on time when we're going out …

Kelley: Oh! Gosh, I'm really sorry. I guess I didn't think it made that much difference …

Paul: Well, sometimes it's not a big deal. But, like tonight, we had a reservation for 7:00. It's already almost 7:30, and the movie starts at 8:45.

Julia: And Carlos still isn't here.

John: You're right. We should try harder to be on time, especially when we need to be somewhere at a specific time. And we should call if something's gonna make us late. Here comes Carlos, by the way. Do you want me to talk to him?

Julia: That'd be great, thanks.

John: Hey Carlos, Kelley and I were just saying that the three of us are usually late when we meet up with Julia and Paul. What can we do to make sure we'll be on time? …

1. Julia asks Paul if they should talk to their friends about being on time.

_____

2. Kelley wants to tell Paul and Julia about something she and John saw.

_____

3. Julia brings up the subject of being late with Kelley and John.

_____

4. John begins to discuss the same topic with Carlos.

_____

B. **LISTENING Rumor has it.** Listen to the information that passes from one person to another in the series of short conversations. Then, listen again for the phrases that begin each conversation. Match those phrases with the information that follows.

_____ **1.** Have you heard …?

_____ **2.** What do you think of this?

_____ **3.** Can you believe this?

_____ **4.** We need to talk about …

_____ **5.** I just heard that …

a. Dave and Shreena are getting married

b. plane tickets are only $150 round-trip

c. you and Dave are getting married

d. airline tickets to Jamaica are cheap

e. what we're doing for spring break

C. **LISTENING What do you think?** Listen to the conversation, paying attention to phrases that introduce topics. Then, write down the phrase you hear that has the same meaning as the phrases to the right.

1. _____

2. _____

3. _____

4. _____

5. _____

wait till you hear

I'd like your opinion about

changing the subject

I can't figure out

we'll want to talk about

Cultural Connections: Text and Phone Etiquette

People often need to get in touch with each other at all times of the day or night. With so many ways to communicate, it is faster and easier than ever to reach people. But just because it's possible to contact people any time, it doesn't mean you always should.

In the United States, it is usually acceptable to call or text message people between 9:00 in the morning and 5:00 in the afternoon. Most people have dinner between 5:30 and 7:30, and it's generally considered rude to call or text during mealtimes. You also should not disturb people early in the morning or late in the evening.

However, younger people tend to have more relaxed views about acceptable hours for receiving texts and phone calls.

Another important consideration in phone and texting etiquette is that the United States has nine different time zones. Be sure that you know what time it is before you try to reach someone in another part of the country.

When is it acceptable to call or text someone where you're from? What are the "rules" of politeness for contacting people?

A: **Listen to this!** The fish populations are actually increasing in the river now.
B: That's great. That water used to be so polluted …

A: **Do you know anything about** being on a jury? I just got a letter telling me to show up for jury duty.
B: Well, I know that a lot of people try to get out of it. But you should do it. It's really an important part of being a citizen.

PHRASES

Can you believe that …?

Did you know that …?

Did you hear (that) / hear about …?

Did you read (that) / read about …?

You know what I just saw / read / heard …?

You'll never guess / believe what I just saw / read / heard.

Look at this / (at) what it says here!

Listen to this / what it says here!

What do / did you think about …?

I'd like your opinion about …

Do you know anything about …?

I don't understand / know why / what / who … (Do you?)

I can't figure out why / what / who … (Can you?)

I was hoping we could talk about …

We need to decide / talk about / discuss …

Speaking of … + *related topic*

Can we change the subject …?

Turning to another topic …

On a (completely) different matter / topic / subject …

Now that you mention it …

Note: See the *Speaker's Handbook* on page 157 for additional phrases.

D. Getting started. For each situation, write down two different ways to start a conversation about the topic.

Example: You want to talk about news you just heard about a colleague.

Did you hear that Alan is leaving the company?

I can't figure out why Alan is leaving the company. Can you?

1. You want to talk about a movie you've just seen.

_____

_____

2. Something you heard earlier doesn't make sense, and you want to talk about it with someone.

_____

_____

3. You want someone's opinion about the clothes you're wearing.

_____

_____

4. You want to tell people something interesting or shocking about a celebrity.

_____

_____

5. You want to get some tips on how to play a certain game.

_____

_____

6. You want to find a student or community organization you could join.

_____

_____

E. Could we talk about …? Write a list of five different topics that you'd like to start a conversation about with your classmates. Then, write some phrases you might use to introduce these topics.

1. _____

2. _____

3. _____

4. _____

5. _____

●● TALK ●●

F. **Peer correction.** Compare the sentences you wrote for each topic in Activity D with those of your classmates. Tell them which of their sentences you like best and why.

G. **Listen to this.** Move around the classroom and have conversations with various classmates. Take turns talking about the topics you listed in Activity E. Be sure to use the phrases you learned to start a conversation.

Example: **A:** *Hey, I finally got around to seeing* Avatar. *You saw it when it first came out, didn't you? What did you think of it?*
B: *I liked it a lot. But I was a little disappointed in the story.*
A: *Me too, I guess. But the story wasn't really the point, was it? It was more about the amazing special effects!*

H. **Look at that!** Have a conversation with a classmate about the subject of each image.

Example: **A:** *I just love parades, don't you?*
B: *I did when I was a kid. But now I just feel like they're a big waste of time and money.*
A: *I don't know. I love seeing the creative things people come up with. And my grandkids really like them.*
B: *That makes sense. Maybe I'll change my mind when I have grandkids.*

1.

Useful Vocabulary

hairdo / bows / outfits /
ridiculous / cute / embarrassing

2.

Useful Vocabulary

air quality / pollution / unhealthy /
breathe / emissions

3.

Useful Vocabulary

to get scared / to scream /
nightmares / special effects

4.

Useful Vocabulary

rough / dangerous / injuries /
damage / competitive

5.

Useful Vocabulary

volunteer / give time / help out /
improvement / community

●● PREPARE ●●

LISTENING COMPREHENSION: *Predicting What's Coming Next*

Long sentences with more than one clause can be difficult to understand. One way to help you follow the meaning of complex sentences is to listen for conjunctions. Conjunctions are words and phrases that show how the parts of a sentence are related. By listening for conjunctions, sometimes you can predict how a two-part sentence will end.

Patricia can't come to the party **because** …

When you hear the conjunction **because**, you can predict that you will hear a reason why Patricia can't come to the party.

Patricia can't come to the party **because** her dad's in the hospital.

Here are other important conjunctions that will help you predict what's coming next.

- **although**   **Although** I don't feel like it, I'll go to the party, …
- **unless**   … but I'm not going **unless** you go too.
- **in case**   I'll take my own car **in case** I want to leave early.
- **as long as**   You can ride with me **as long as** you leave when I do.
- **since**   **Since** I'm going, I'd better bring something.
- **so (that)**   We should go early **so that** we can help set up.

CD 1
Tracks
22-23

I. LISTENING **Are we going or not?** Listen to the conversation. You will hear several pauses after conjunctions. During each pause, decide which phrase most logically completes the sentence, and circle **a** or **b**. Then, listen to the complete conversation to check your answers.

1. **a.** I can let David know.
   b. I can buy our plane tickets.

2. **a.** … it's a nice day.
   b. … it rains.

3. **a.** I see some dark clouds out there.
   b. … the sun is shining, and the temperature is perfect.

4. **a.** I wish I could go on one every week in the summer!
   b. I do not want to be outside in bad weather.

5. **a.** … we have plenty of time to think about it later.
   b. … we're supposed to bring a dessert.

CD 1
Track
24

J. LISTENING **A case of nerves.** Listen to the conversation. You will hear five unfinished sentences. Based on the conjunction you hear, write an ending to each sentence that makes sense.

1. Ms. Shaw, please tell me your feelings so that _____

2. Knock it off unless _____

3. And since you're an English major, _____

4. You have to stop thinking about him because _____

5. I'll give Andre a try, as long as _____

Aron: Well, **the important thing is that** the date went well.

Ted: Yeah, but she should've contacted me again by now, **don't you think?**

Aron: **Have you thought about** the possibility that she's waiting to see what you do?

Ted: **What do you mean?**

Aron: I mean maybe you should call *her*! **Like I said**, the date went well, right?

Ted: **Good point. On the other hand,** I don't want to look too desperate.

PHRASES

Emphasizing Important Information

There's (just) one thing.

In the first place, …

Two / three things. First, … (Second, … / Third, …)

The important thing is (that) …

What really matters is (that) …

Sharing Opinions

I think that …

Do / Don't you think that …?

What do *you* think?

Don't you think (so)?

Do you agree?

You're making a good point.

That's a good point.

Seeking Clarification

What do you mean (by that)?

I don't get / understand what you're saying.

Could you give me / us an example?

Offering Another Point of View

What about …? / Have you thought about …?

On the other hand, …

In addition, …

Keeping Focused

Let's stay on topic.

We're getting off track here.

To answer / get back to your question, …

Summarizing

Like I said (before), …

In conclusion, …

So, to sum things up, …

Note: See the *Speaker's Handbook* on page 157 for additional phrases.

K. **What's missing?** The staff of an adult education program is planning a workshop to help people fill out their income tax forms. Read their discussion. Fill in each blank with an appropriate phrase from the **Communicative Strategies** to complete the conversation.

Brad: Everyone needs to do taxes. That's why I think this workshop will be so helpful.

Jaime: Remember the workshop we did on taking care of babies? We had all those toy baby dolls, and—

Brad: *(interrupting)* Hold on, Jaime. We can share stories later. Right now we have to think about this workshop on tax forms.

Jaime: Right. Sorry, _____. So you were saying that first we should
(1)
make a list of the skills our presenters need to have.

Suzanne: I'm not sure I follow you. _____?
(2)

Brad: OK, for example, we'll need a few tax experts who can explain all the forms. And it might be good to have some translators there too—maybe Spanish and Portuguese. _____?
(3)

Anne: _____, because some people who come to our workshops
(4)
don't understand English very well.

Brad: So, we still have a few details to settle. But _____ is that we
(5)
make sure all the people who attend get the help they need.

Jaime: This is such a good idea. But _____ the fact that not
(6)
everyone can come at night? Is that a problem?

Brad: What if we did it twice—once during the day and once in the evening?

Suzanne: _____ we should as long as the presenters can be at both
(7)
sessions. _____ Anne?
(8)

Anne: I agree. So, _____ first, let's line up the people we need right
(9)
now. And second, let's decide the date and times.

Suzanne: I have one more question. When you say, "People will pay on a sliding scale," _____, exactly?
(10)

Brad: Sorry. That means that the people who earn less will pay less. It's only fair. …

L. Pros and cons. Make a list of pros (reasons for) and cons (reasons against) for getting a master's degree after college. In your list, include phrases from the **Communicative Strategies** that you could use when having a conversation about this topic.

Getting a Master's Degree

Pros	Cons

M. Brainstorming. Read the topics. Then, write five words or expressions that you might use in a discussion about each topic.

Example: an inexpensive, fun vacation

relax	*easy*	*interesting*
save money	*peaceful*	

1. keeping wild animals in zoos

_____ _____ _____

_____ _____

2. things that people will and won't do to save energy

_____ _____ _____

_____ _____

3. whether it's OK to eat fast food

_____ _____ _____

_____ _____

4. whether young children should have pets

_____ _____ _____

_____ _____

Professional Context: Discussions in Meetings

In professional settings, meetings usually involve more formal discussions. People who lead the meetings often state formally what the purpose or the goal is.

The purpose of this meeting is to …
Today we need to …
I've called this meeting so we can …

It's also common to follow a printed agenda that is distributed before the meeting begins. The agenda states in writing what topics will be discussed and in what order. The person who calls the meeting takes responsibility for following the agenda.

The first item on our agenda is …
Now let's move on to …
Let's table (postpone) this for now and return to it next time.

Usually, someone at the meeting takes notes, or *minutes*, on what is shared or decided. The minutes are usually typed and sent to the participants after the meeting is over.

 TALK

N. Peer correction. Compare the pros and cons you used in Activity L with those of your classmates. Write down some new ideas that you hadn't put in your lists.

O. Is it a good idea? Talk about the pros and cons you came up with in Activity L with a classmate. Use the phrases for managing a discussion and the reasons from your lists.

Example: **A:** *I think that it's important to get a master's degree so that you can get a better job. Do you agree?*

B: *That's a good point, but have you thought about how expensive it is to go back to school? …*

Language Focus: Tag questions

A "tag question" is sometimes added at the end of a statement to check whether you're right or to invite people to agree with you.

You all agree with me, **don't you**?   He's not listening, **is he**?

Two common types of tag questions:

1. In statements with action verbs, the tag question uses the form of **do** that agrees with the subject.

   He knows all about this, **doesn't he**?   You don't think I'm right, **do you**?

2. In statements with the verb *to be*, the tag question uses the form of *to be* that agrees with the subject.

   You're not confused, **are you**?   She's right, **isn't she**?

Note:

- When your statement is affirmative, your tag question should be negative, and vice versa.
- In affirmative statements with *I am*, the tag question is *aren't I?*

   I'm getting off track, **aren't I**?

P. Word bank. Compare the words and phrases you wrote down for Activity M with those of your classmates. Add to your own list any additional words you hear about each topic.

Q. On the other hand … Discuss the topics from Activity M with a classmate. Use the phrases you learned in the **Communicative Strategies** and the words you wrote down to guide your conversation.

Example: keeping wild animals in zoos
   A: *I think keeping wild animals in zoos is important to protect them. Do you agree?*
   B: *No, I don't agree. In the first place, some zoos are pretty bad at taking care of the animals. In addition, the animals seem bored sitting around in their cages all day. It's not even their natural habitat!*
   A: *That's a good point. But on the other hand, zoos are important for protecting endangered species, aren't they? …*

R. What do you think? Choose one of the following subjects to discuss with your classmates. One member of your group should take notes. When your discussion is finished, summarize your conversation for the rest of the class.

1. You have $200 to spend on a party for your class. How will you spend the money in a way that everyone will enjoy? Decide who will take care of which arrangements for the party.

2. You volunteer in an elementary school where one child has been bullying another. Discuss what should be done to solve this problem.

3. Your friend is a student and lives in a city that has a good bus system. Even so, he or she would like to buy a car. Discuss whether or not this is a good idea.

●● IMPROVISE ●●

CD 1
Track
25
S. **LISTENING** **Cultural differences.** Three friends are talking about their sociology class, but their conversation goes off in another direction. Listen to the conversation and answer the following questions about the **Communicative Strategies** they use.

1. What phrases does the second speaker, Arin, use to bring up a new topic?

2. Later in the conversation, the same speaker brings the discussion back to the main topic. What phrases does she use?

3. The other speakers, Cathy and Brian, both ask for clarification during the conversation. What phrases do they use?

4. What phrase does Arin use to give an opinion? What phrase does she use to ask for an opinion?

5. What conclusions can you draw about Arin, Cathy, and Brian based on how they manage this conversation?

T. **Ethical question.** With your classmates, discuss whether you approve or disapprove of using animals in scientific research. Your teacher will give each of you a card that describes the role you play in the discussion.

U. **Talk show.** With a group of classmates, role-play a talk show in which you discuss one of the topics below. The "host" introduces the topic, asks questions, and keeps people focused on the discussion. The "guests" give opinions, explain their points of view, and give examples to support their ideas. When the discussion ends, the rest of the class (the audience) identifies the phrases they heard from the **Communicative Strategies**.

1. Should young adults be able to drink alcohol at the age of 18?

2. Do professional athletes make too much money?

3. Should boys and girls go to separate schools?

V. **Class discussion.** Discuss the following question with the whole class: *What do people of different generations have in common?* Think about your own interactions with people older and younger than you. Use phrases from the **Communicative Strategies** for managing a discussion.

INTERNET RESEARCH **Online discussions.** Go online and find blogs or discussions that deal with a topic that interests you. Take notes about the various opinions that people express. Write down some ways that they introduce topics and keep the discussions going. In what ways are these online discussions similar to spoken conversations? In what ways are they different?

3 Giving Instructions

"The first thing you do is …"

Strategies for Communication

Part 1: How to Ask for Instructions

Part 2: How to Give Instructions

Part One

 PREPARE

A. PRE-LISTENING How do I do this? Check off (✔) the activities for which you personally would need instructions.

_____ setting an alarm clock	_____ playing mahjong
_____ riding a bicycle	_____ changing camera batteries
_____ ordering a book on the Internet	_____ using a washing machine
_____ doing a crossword puzzle	_____ tying a shoelace
_____ writing a paper for class	_____ buying a gift for someone
_____ planting a garden	_____ slicing vegetables
_____ swimming	_____ organizing a garage sale
_____ drawing a cat	_____ taking care of a dog
_____ playing basketball	_____ using the library
_____ finding volunteer work	_____ finding a job

CD 1 ◀))) **B. LISTENING What and how?** Listen to each set of instructions. Write down what
Tracks people are learning to do.
26–31

1. how to _____   **4.** how to _____

2. how to _____   **5.** how to _____

3. how to _____   **6.** how to _____

CD 1 ◀))) **C. LISTENING How to …** Listen to the conversation. Write down the words and phrases
Track you hear that are helpful in giving instructions.
32

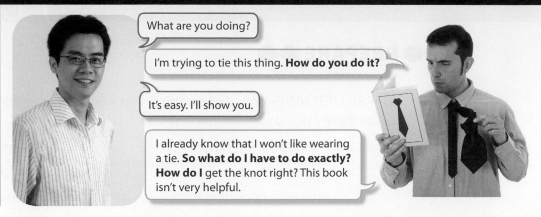

What are you doing?

I'm trying to tie this thing. **How do you do it?**

It's easy. I'll show you.

I already know that I won't like wearing a tie. **So what do I have to do exactly? How do I** get the knot right? This book isn't very helpful.

PHRASES

Asking what something is

What is this? / What's that?

What are these things? / What are those?

What is this thing? / What's that gadget / gizmo?

Is this a . . . ?

Can you tell me what this is?

Do you know what this is?

Likely responses

It's a . . .

They're . . .

It's a . . .

Yes, it is. / No, it isn't. It's a . . .

I think it's a . . .

Yes, I do. It's a . . . / No, I don't.

Asking what something is for

What's this used for?

What are these (things) for?

What do you do with this thing / gadget / gizmo?

What does this (thing / gadget / gizmo) do?

Can you tell me / Do you know what this is for?

Likely responses

It's used to / for . . .

You use them to / for . . .

It's a . . . You . . .

It . . .

I'm not sure. / I don't know.

Asking how something works

How does this (thing / gadget / gizmo) work?

How do I make this / it work?

How do I / you . . . ?

What is / What's the best way to . . . ?

How do I go about . . . ?

Can you tell / show me how to . . . ?

What is / What's the first thing I need to do?

Do you know how to . . . ?

Language Focus: Verbs Related to How Things Work

Below is a selection of common verbs you might use in combination with phrases to ask how something works.

Examples: *Do you know how to **eject** the CD?*
*How do I **use** this washing machine?*

		Related to technology
to attach	to repair	
to close	to start	to copy
to detach	to stop	to download
to fix	to turn	to eject
to install	to turn off	to highlight
to open	to turn on	to post
to plug in	to unplug	to print
to push (a button)	to use	to put in

D. **What's this?** Use the phrases from the **Communicative Strategies** to ask what something is. Look at the answers to help you decide how to ask the question.

Example: **A:** What's this?
           B: I think it's a wireless adapter.

1. A: _____

    B: I don't know. I think it's something you use with the camera.

2. A: _____

    B: It's the thing that connects the TV to the cable box.

3. A: _____

    B: That? It's a kind of screwdriver.

4. A: _____

    B: They're bulbs for the flashlight.

5. A: _____

    B: I'm not sure. But I think it's a juicer for fruits and vegetables.

6. A: _____

    B: It's a spice used in Indian food.

E. What is it and what's it for? Look at the objects in the pictures. Write questions you would ask someone to find out what the objects are and what they're used for. Use the phrases from the **Communicative Strategies**.

1. _____
   _____
   _____

2. _____
   _____
   _____

3. _____
   _____
   _____

4. _____
   _____
   _____

5. _____
   _____
   _____

6. _____
   _____
   _____

F. **How do I ...?** Write a question using a phrase from the **Communicative Strategies** and an appropriate verb to ask how each of the following objects works. You will compare your questions with those of your classmates.

Example:

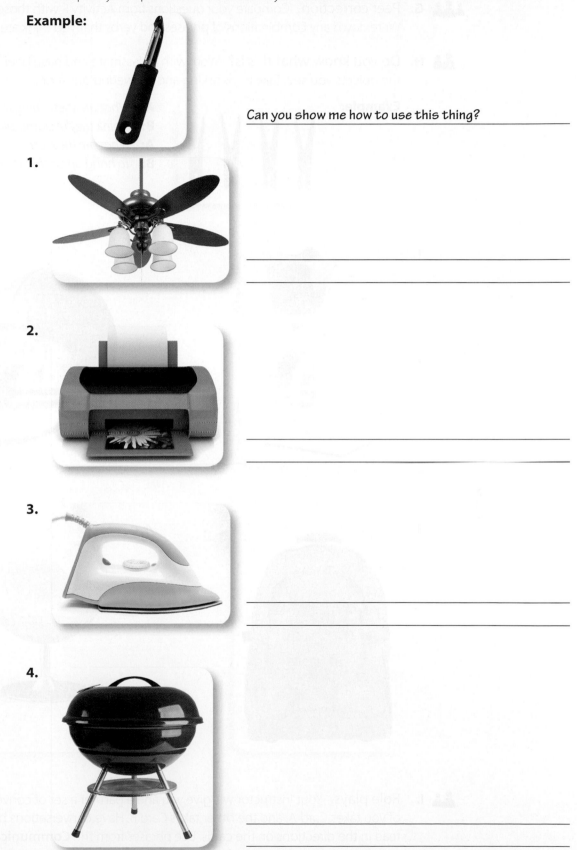

Can you show me how to use this thing?

1.

2.

3.

4.

TALK

G. Peer correction. Compare your questions from Activity F with those of your classmates. Write down any combinations of phrases and verbs that you think are interesting.

H. Do you know what this is? Work with a classmate and have brief conversations about the objects you see. Take turns asking and answering questions.

Example:

A: *What are these things?*
B: *I think they're clothespins.*
A: *What are they for?*
B: *To hang up clothes to dry on a line outside.*

1.

2.

3.

4.

I. Role plays. Your instructor will give you and a partner a set of conversation cards. One of you takes Card A, and the other takes Card B. Have conversations based on what you read in the directions on the cards. Use phrases from the **Communicative Strategies**.

 **PREPARE** ●●

LISTENING COMPREHENSION: _Understanding Instructions_

When someone gives you instructions to do something, the details matter. That means it's important to listen carefully for the exact information that's being given to you.

- Listen for sequence words and phrases: **first (second, third)**, **then**, **next**, **before that**, **after that**, **finally**, and so on. Sequence words help you understand the order of the instructions.
- Listen for action verbs: **plug in**, **disconnect**, **turn on**, **push the button**, **open**, **close**, **attach**, and so on. Action verbs in instructions tell you what you have to do.
- Listen for specific objects, such as **outlet**, **wires**, **cables**, **batteries**, and so on. Objects in instructions tell you what you should be working with.

If you're still not sure you heard the instructions correctly, you should ask for clarification.

CD 1 🔊))
Tracks
33–36

J. LISTENING **What are the steps?** Listen to each set of instructions. Number the steps of the instructions in the correct order.

1. _____ Select the water temperature.

_____ Start the dishwasher.

_____ Close the door.

_____ Put the soap into the compartment.

2. _____ Turn the table top upside down on the floor.

_____ Get the right tools.

_____ Make sure you have all the table pieces.

_____ Read the instructions.

_____ Screw the legs into the table top.

3. _____ Turn on the camera.

_____ Connect the camera to the computer.

4. _____ Cut up the onions and vegetables.

_____ Melt some butter in a frying pan.

_____ Take the eggs out of the refrigerator.

_____ Cook the vegetables.

_____ Stir the eggs.

_____ Scramble the eggs with the vegetables.

_____ Add some salt and pepper to the eggs.

CD 1
Tracks
33–36

K. LISTENING **Important details.** Listen to the four sets of instructions again. Write the action verbs you hear that give the instructions.

1. _____

2. _____

3. _____

4. _____

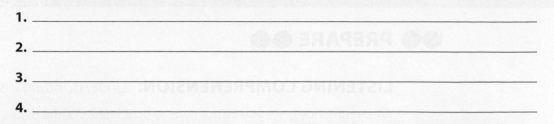

COMMUNICATIVE STRATEGIES: *How to Give Instructions*

You can learn how to draw a frog in just four steps. These instructions and drawings take you through each step. Use a pencil, follow the red lines shown in each step, and you'll end up with a frog that looks like this.

To begin with, you draw the body, the head, the eyes, and the legs. First, you draw two egg shapes: one slightly smaller than the other. Then, you draw two circles for the eyes. You add two football shapes on either side of the bigger egg shape for the legs.

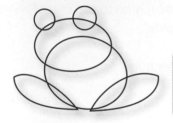

The next step is to draw the feet. You draw the back feet under the two football shapes and add curved lines through the center of them. Then, you add the arm shapes.

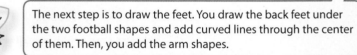

In the third step, you draw in the details: shaded circles for the center of the eyes and different sized circles for the spots on the skin. Then, you draw the front feet with three toes. After that, you add a wavy line for the mouth and curved lines for the eyebrows and to finish the back feet.

Finally, you trace over the lines you want to keep with a pen, and you erase the extra ones. Good work! You've drawn a frog!

Giving Instructions

This is what you do. / Here's what you do.

Beginning

Before you begin, you should / you may want to …

First, you …

The first step is to … / The first thing you (need to) do is …

You should probably start by …

I would start by …

The best place to start is …

To begin with …

Continuing

Then, you …

The next step is to …

Once / When you've done that, then …

The next thing you do is …

After that, you …

Ending

Finally, you …

The last thing (you do) is …

Asking for Clarification

What did you say?

What do I do?

Did you say …?

How am I supposed to …?

How / Which way does this go?

What do I do first?

Wait, I didn't hear you / catch that.

Hold on a minute. Can you say that again?

Slow down. You're going too fast. What was that?

There are two verb forms you can use when giving instructions: the imperative and the present tense.

The imperative form is the same as when you give commands: **go**, **start**, **copy**, **disconnect**. The present tense in instructions is always stated in the second person (you): **you go**, **you copy**, **you disconnect**.

> Imperative: To get to the library, **go** down this street and then **turn** left.
>
> Present tense: To get to the library, **you go** down this street and then **you turn** left.

Generally, you use the imperative more often when giving instructions to children. With adults, you can use either the imperative or the present tense.

L. Giving instructions. Write sentences using phrases from the **Communicative Strategies** and the prompts provided. You can use either the imperative or the present tense or mix the two.

Example: turn on the computer / insert a blank CD / wait for the prompts
First, (you) turn on the computer. Then, (you) insert a blank CD. Once you've done that, (you) wait for the prompts.

1. go up two blocks / turn right / walk to the next light / cross the street to the office building

_____

_____

_____

2. load the dishes / put the silverware into the basket / add the soap / close the dishwasher / push this button to turn it on

_____

_____

_____

3. take two pieces of bread / butter one side of each piece / put cheese and ham on the side that's not buttered / close the sandwich / cook it in a skillet or under the broiler until the cheese melts

_____

_____

_____

4. bring up the mahjong tiles on the computer / to eliminate the tiles, click on each of two matching symbols / keep doing this until you have no tiles left

_____

_____

_____

5. decide how many classes you want to take / count the number of required courses / look at the list of courses / choose the electives that interest you

_____

_____

_____

Professional Context: Giving Instructions

In professional settings, there are basically two situations in which you give instructions: (1) when teaching something to a group, and (2) when teaching an individual.

When you're giving instructions to a group, it's acceptable to be very direct and use the imperative.

> OK, everyone. **First, click** on the flag icon to open the spreadsheet. **Next, type** your name at the top. **Now, add** the tasks you completed in each row.

When you're working with individuals, you're more likely to use indirect language in order to be more polite.

> OK, **the first thing you need to do is click** on the flag icon to get into the spreadsheet. **Once you open it, you're going to type** your name at the top. **Now, you can add** the tasks you completed in each row.

M. **This is what you do.** Think of something you would want to teach your classmates how to do. Write a set of instructions that explains each step in the process. If your instructor agrees, bring an object that helps you explain the instructions. Search the Internet for ideas to help you explain the steps. Remember to use phrases from the **Communicative Strategies** in your instructions.

Possible Instructions

how to draw something **/** how to play a sport **/** how to cook something (recipe) **/** how to play a game **/** how to change the batteries in something **/** how to order something on the Internet **/** how to use an appliance **/** how to build something **/** how to print a document **/** how to use a camera **/** how to play a video game

●● TALK ●●

N. **This is what you do.** Move around the room and explain to three different classmates how to do the activity you selected and prepared in Activity M. Remember to use phrases from the **Communicative Strategies** in your explanations. Ask others for clarification as you listen to their instructions. Take notes so that you can give their instructions to another classmate in Activity O.

Cultural Connections: Teaching Styles

In English, the word *instruction* is often used to mean the same thing as the word *teaching*. People who teach—at home, at school, or in business—instruct others about what to learn, how to learn it, and why it should be learned.

Every teacher has his or her own teaching style. Some use direct and indirect commands and expect all students to follow the same instructions (teacher-centered). Others teach more through suggestion, giving students the freedom to learn the way they want to (student-centered). A third approach is to mix the two styles depending on what you're teaching. How you're taught—or instructed— influences how you learn and how you give instructions to others.

How were you taught by teachers and family members in the past? How much freedom did you have in choosing what to learn and how to learn it? What influence did someone's teaching style have on you?

O. **What I learned.** In Activity N, you learned how to do things from three of your classmates. Now teach another classmate about one thing you learned how to do. For example, if you got instructions about how to draw an animal, teach your classmate how to do the same thing.

👥 **P.** **Interesting objects.** Imagine that a time traveler from 200 years ago visits us in the present and has never seen the most common objects we use today. With a classmate, role-play this situation and have conversations about the objects shown. Use phrases for giving instructions.

Example:

A: *What's this thing?*

B: *It's a dishwasher.*

A: *What's it for?*

B: *It's used to wash plates and silverware and other utensils.*

A: *How does it work?*

B: *First, you load the dishes in the baskets. Then, you put soap in this compartment. After that, you close the door and push this button to start it. An hour later, your dishes are washed and you can use them again.*

1.

2.

3.

4.

5.

6.

 **IMPROVISE**

CD 1
Tracks
37–38

Q. LISTENING What are they talking about? Listen to two sets of instructions. Then, answer the questions for each set.

Instructions 1

1. Who is probably talking?

2. What's the general topic?

3. What specific instructions are given?

4. What's the first thing you should do before anything else?

5. What's the very last thing you should do?

6. How many times a day should you do this?

Instructions 2

7. What instructions are given?

8. What are the main ingredients?

9. What ingredients need to be cooked?

10. How is this meal going to be served?

R. How do you …? As a class, talk about what you see in each photograph. Discuss how it works, how it's made, what you do with it, or when you usually see it. Use the phrases you've learned in this chapter for asking and giving instructions.

Example: **A:** *What's that?*
B: *It's a game called pool.*
C: *How do you play it?*
B: *You use the long sticks to hit a white ball on a table. The white ball rolls and hits other colored balls. You try to knock the colored balls into holes along the edge of the table, but you only hit the white ball. If there are two players, one player tries to hit in seven solid color balls, and the other player has to hit in the seven striped balls.*
D: *How do you win the game?*
B: *After you hit all your balls into the holes, then you try to hit in the black 8 ball. The first person to do that wins the game.*

1.

2.

3.

4. **5.** **6.**

👥👥 **S.** **Puzzles.** With your classmates, guess what the following objects are, what they're for, and how they're used. Use the phrases you've learned in the chapter, and ask for clarification if there's something you don't understand. If you can't figure out one of the objects, ask another group if they know.

1. **2.** **3.**

4. **5.** **6.**

🖱️ **INTERNET RESEARCH How do you ...?** Many sites on the Internet give step-by-step instructions on how to do things—for example, paper folding (origami), drawing, fixing a toilet, using a kayak, and so on. Think of something you'd like to learn to do, and search online for the instructions on how to do it. Then, give the instructions to your classmates. Use the phrases you learned in this chapter to ask for and give instructions.

4 Talking about the News

"Did you know that …?"

●● PREPARE ●●

A. **PRE-LISTENING You and the news.** Answer the questions about how you find out what's happening in the world.

1. Is it important to know what's going on in the world? Why or why not?

_____

_____

2. When in your daily life is it important to know about news events? For classes? For work? In conversations? Explain why.

_____

_____

3. How do you get your news? From TV? From newspapers? From magazines? From radio? From the Internet? From other people? All of these?

_____

_____

4. What times of the day do you usually get your news?

_____

_____

5. What kinds of news are you most interested in? Why?

_____

_____

CD 1 **B.** **LISTENING What section of the newspaper?** Listen to each of the short exchanges
Tracks and write down the section of the newspaper in which the news item is likely to be
39-46 found. Some sections might be used more than once and others not at all.

Newspaper sections:
book review / business / entertainment / food / health /
international / politics / society / sports / technology / travel

Conversation 1: _____   **Conversation 5:** _____

Conversation 2: _____   **Conversation 6:** _____

Conversation 3: _____   **Conversation 7:** _____

Conversation 4: _____   **Conversation 8:** _____

C. LISTENING A piece of news. Listen to three conversations. Write down any phrases you hear that the people use to bring up a piece of news or to ask for additional information.

Conversation 1

_____

_____

_____

_____

_____

Conversation 2

_____

_____

_____

_____

_____

Conversation 3

_____

_____

_____

_____

_____

COMMUNICATIVE STRATEGIES: *How to Start Talking about a News Item*

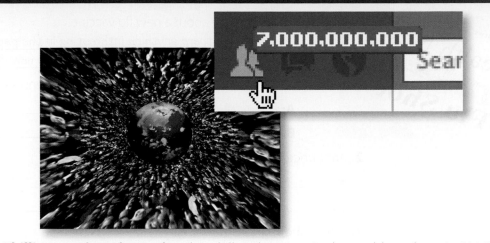

Phillip: **Did you know that** the 7 billionth person in the world was born in 2011?
Lydia: Where did you hear that?
Phillip: **It says so right here** on this website.
Lydia: **What does it say about** the problem of overpopulation?
Phillip: **It just mentions** the impact on world hunger.

PHRASES

Starting the Conversation

I just saw / read / heard that …

I just read / heard about …

Listen to this.

Did you know that …?

Have you heard about …?

Do you know (anything about) …?

Is / Was there anything interesting in the news / in the paper?

Anything interesting in the paper (in the news)?

What does / did it say about …?

Is there anything new about …?

What's the latest about …?

By the way, have you heard anything about …?

Do you know what's happening with …?

What's new about / with …?

Have you heard / read about …?

Did you hear any more / anything else about …?

Responding

Yes … / No …

All it says is that …

It says here that …

They say that …

It says so right here.

It just mentions (that) …

From what I heard / read, …

According to what it says here / what I heard …,

Note: See the *Speaker's Handbook* on page 157 for additional phrases.

D. Have you heard? Read each news topic. Write one sentence to start a conversation about the topic and one sentence to respond. Use phrases from the **Communicative Strategies**.

Example: article about a new flu vaccine

A: Is there anything interesting in the paper?

B: Yeah. It says here that there's a new flu vaccine.

1. article about Vanessa Ross, the winner of a tennis tournament

A: _____

B: _____

2. announcement about a new piece of technology

A: _____

B: _____

3. article about global warming

A: _____

B: _____

4. announcement by Marta Gonzalez that she is running for governor

A: _____

B: _____

5. announcement about the opening of a new coffee shop

A: _____

B: _____

6. article about a car crash

A: _____

B: _____

7. article about a crime

A: _____

B: _____

8. article about the publication of a new book

A: _____

B: _____

E. News items. Look through a newspaper or browse an online news website. Read five news items and write down the topic(s) covered in each one.

1. _____

2. _____

3. _____

4. _____

5. _____

F. **A news story I read.** Now choose one of the news stories (print or online) from Activity E and write down the main ideas of the article. Also jot down some phrases from the **Communicative Strategies** for starting a conversation about the news. You'll talk about this article with one of your classmates.

Cultural Connections: Objectivity in News Reporting

Objectivity means presenting a situation using only facts, not opinions. In the United States, news organizations often say that they report their news objectively. However, many people believe it's not possible for journalists to set aside their own beliefs and feelings about events. They think the news media is biased, or more in favor of one side of the facts than other sides. Many American newspapers, radio stations, and TV news stations represent a certain point of view (liberal, conservative, religious, etc.). To find real objectivity in the news, you should refer to several news sources to get all sides of the story.

How do people feel about the accuracy of the news where you're from? Is it believed that reported news is objective and without bias? Why or why not?

●● TALK ●●

G. **Peer correction.** Share with your classmates the sentences you wrote in Activity D. Point out any mistakes you hear and make corrections to your sentences if needed.

H. **News items.** Move around the room and have conversations with several classmates about the news items you wrote down in Activity E. When someone begins a conversation with you about a news item, respond appropriately and add logical details (even if they're made up). Use phrases from the **Communicative Strategies**.

I. **An article I read.** Tell a classmate about the article you read in Activity F. Your classmate can ask for clarification and additional information. Use phrases from the **Communicative Strategies**.

Part Two

LISTENING COMPREHENSION *Understanding Details in a News Story*

One of the basic principles of a news story is that it should include answers to some or all of the following six questions:

Who?	→	Listen for names, titles, groups of people
What?	→	Listen for the topic, people's actions
Where?	→	Listen for names of places, location words
How?	→	Listen for how something happened (or was accomplished)
When?	→	Listen for dates, times, years, time words
Why?	→	Listen for reasons, explanations

- The order that these questions are addressed depends on the story.
- Not every news story answers all of these questions.
- Some of the questions have more than one answer in a news story.

CD 1 ◀))) **J.** LISTENING **One question at a time.** Select the one *major* question (**who, what,**
Tracks **where, how, when, why**) that's being answered in each news segment.
50-55

1. _____ 3. _____ 5. _____

2. _____ 4. _____ 6. _____

CD 1 ◀))) **K.** LISTENING **I just heard …** Listen to the radio news report and answer the questions.
Track
56

1. What is this story about? _____

_____

2. Who is this story about? _____

3. What happened? _____

_____

4. How did it happen? _____

_____

5. Where did it happen? _____

6. When did it happen? _____

7. Why did it happen? _____

8. What's the secondary topic of the news story? _____

9. What does the news story say about American television viewing? _____

_____

_____

10. What three questions are asked at the end of the news story? _____

_____

_____

Professional Context: Keeping up with the News

For many business professionals, knowing what's going on in the world is important for their jobs. To stay informed quickly, people often skim (read for the main ideas) and scan (read for supporting details) print and online news stories. It is common to see businesspeople glued to their portable electronic devices, such as smartphones and laptops, in order to follow the latest news (especially financial news) that applies to their work. If you have any interest in business, you will probably need to be in the habit of keeping up with the news.

COMMUNICATIVE STRATEGIES: *How to Discuss the News*

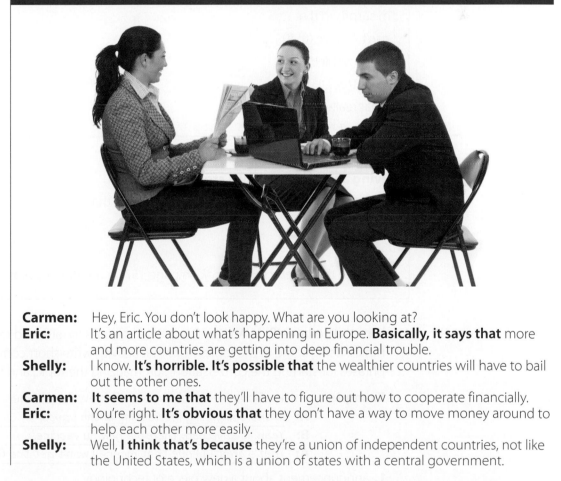

Carmen: Hey, Eric. You don't look happy. What are you looking at?

Eric: It's an article about what's happening in Europe. **Basically, it says that** more and more countries are getting into deep financial trouble.

Shelly: I know. **It's horrible. It's possible that** the wealthier countries will have to bail out the other ones.

Carmen: **It seems to me that** they'll have to figure out how to cooperate financially.

Eric: You're right. **It's obvious that** they don't have a way to move money around to help each other more easily.

Shelly: Well, **I think that's because** they're a union of independent countries, not like the United States, which is a union of states with a central government.

Summarizing a story

The article / story is about …

To make a long story short, this is about …

To summarize, …

Basically, it says that …

Reacting to a story

That's / This is / It's / It was + *adjective*

amazing	fabulous	interesting	surprising
awful	great	odd	touching
bizarre	happy	sad	unbelievable
crazy	horrible	strange	wonderful
excellent	incredible	super	worrisome

I didn't know that …

It's obvious / clear that …

It's possible that …

Maybe that means that …

I'm surprised that …

I can't believe (that) …

Unbelievable!

Is that true?

Is that really what it says?

That can't be!

Well, it's about time!

Giving an opinion about a story

It seems to me that … / I think that … / I believe that …

In my opinion …

It's probably because …

Note: See the *Speaker's Handbook* on page 157 for additional phrases.

L. **What's the latest?** In Activity D, you used phrases to raise and respond to a variety of topics. Using some of the topics from that activity, write short conversations that include phrases for starting the conversation, summarizing the topic, and reacting to it.

Example: article about the development of a new flu vaccine

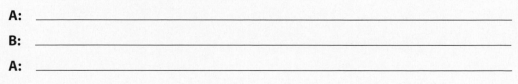

A: Is there anything interesting in the paper?

B: Yeah. It says here there's a new flu vaccine.

A: That's great! I hope that means I won't get the flu this year.

1. announcement about a new piece of technology

A: _____

B: _____

A: _____

2. article about global warming

A: _____

B: _____

A: _____

3. announcement about the opening of a new coffee shop

A: _____

B: _____

A: _____

4. article about a car crash

A: _____

B: _____

A: _____

5. article about a crime

A: _____

B: _____

A: _____

Language Focus: Using Adjectives in Reactions

As shown in the **Communicative Strategies**, adjectives are an important part of reacting to a news story or to the people associated with it. Adjectives of reaction can communicate neutral, positive, or negative feelings.

Neutral adjectives don't reveal in an obvious way how the speaker feels about the topic. These adjectives are helpful when trying to avoid taking a position on the topic: *interesting, fascinating, unusual, original*, etc.

> **The writer of this article has some *original* ideas.**
> *(The adjective doesn't indicate if the speaker agrees or disagrees with the ideas.)*

Positive adjectives make the speaker's feelings very clear. These adjectives show favor for what is said about the topic: *excellent, touching, fabulous, great, sensible, intelligent, good*, etc.

> **I just read a *great* article about global warming.**
> *(The speaker obviously agrees with the content of the article.)*

Negative adjectives also make the speaker's feelings very clear, but those feelings about the news story are negative. These adjectives show that the speaker is not in favor of what is said about the topic: *bad, weird, bizarre, crazy, strange, ridiculous, stupid, flawed, dated, biased, worrisome*, etc.

> **This article is *stupid*. The writer doesn't understand the problem.**
> *(There is no doubt that the speaker has a very low opinion of the writer.)*

Negative adjectives suggest that the speaker has an attitude of superiority. It's best to avoid these types of adjectives in professional contexts or when talking about cultural issues unless you know the listener very well.

M. World population. Read the newspaper article. Then, prepare to talk about it with your classmates by supplying the details requested below. Include phrases from the **Communicative Strategies**.

Our (over)crowded planet: 7 billion people

The year 2011 witnessed a major milestone for a crowded planet Earth.

According to estimates from the United Nations, the 7 billionth baby on the planet was born on October 31, 2011. Because births and deaths are constantly occuring everywhere in the world, it is impossible to know which baby born on that day filled the Earth with its 7 billionth inhabitant. But that didn't stop countries from Nigeria to India to the Philippines from claiming the landmark birth.

Although the birth of a child is usually a cause for celebration, the arrival of the 7 billionth child was equally a cause for concern. Questions were renewed of how the Earth can support the lives of so many people, even with the most basic needs of shelter and food. United Nations Secretary-General Ban Ki-moon noted that this event was "not about one newborn or even one generation" but "about our entire human family."

When you consider the statistics, that family has grown at an extremely fast rate.

The world population officially hit 1 billion in 1804. It took 123 years for that number to double to 2 billion (1927). But since then, the earth has added another billion people in less than a generation: in 32 years to 3 billion (1959); 15 years to reach 4 billion (1974); 13 years later at 5 billion (1987); and only 11 years to reach 6 billion (1998).

With 13 years passing between 6 and 7 billion, population growth appears to be slowing. The United Nations seems to agree, as it has predicted the world population to reach 8 billion by 2025 (after 14 years) and 9 billion by 2043 (after 18 years).

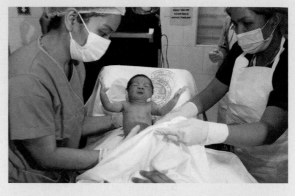

Danica Camacho from the Philippines was one of many babies around the world born on October 31, 2011, who represented the 7 billionth person on Earth.

Even with population growth slowing, the problem remains that the most growth is happening in the least developed parts of the world. By 2050, India will have the highest population of any country, passing China. The United States will be the only developed nation among the 10 most populated.

The concerns about a rising population are numerous: growing economic inequality, wars that result from such inequality, famine, disease, lack of clean water, pollution, and energy shortages.

"We can no longer ignore the reality that our planet has limited resources," said one U.N. source. "We all share in the responsibility of safe-guarding not only our human family but all of the resources that sustain life on this overcrowded planet."

1. three phrases to start the conversation: _____
_____

2. one phrase to summarize, followed by a short summary of the article: _____
_____

3. supporting details in the article:
What? _____
When? _____
Who? _____
Where? _____
How? _____
_____
Why? _____

4. two problems raised in the article: _____
_____

5. your reaction to and opinion about the facts in the article: _____
_____
_____

N. Infamous hijacker. Read the newspaper article. Then, prepare to talk about it with your classmates by supplying the details requested below. Include phrases from the **Communicative Strategies**.

Could family ties solve 40-year hijacking mystery?

An Oklahoma woman remembers Thanksgiving 1971 when one of her uncles showed up at her grandmother's house bloody and bruised. That family memory could help investigators solve one of the most mysterious criminal cases in U.S. history.

Marla Cooper believes that her uncle, Lynn Doyle Cooper, was the infamous D.B. Cooper, a man who hijacked a Northwest Orient Airlines flight in 1971 and got away with $200,000 in ransom money. The Federal Bureau of Investigation has not been able to gather enough evidence in over 40 years to solve the crime, making it the nation's only unsolved hijacking.

Marla Cooper, who was eight years old in 1971, recalls the day before Thanksgiving at her grandmother's house in Sisters, Oregon, when her two uncles were planning something "very mischievous," she told ABC News.

"I was watching them using some very expensive walkie-talkies that they had purchased," she said. "They left to supposedly go turkey hunting, and Thanksgiving morning I was waiting for them to return."

The hijacking took place on November 24, the day before Thanksgiving, on the Northwest Orient plane that took off from Portland, Oregon. A man who called himself Dan Cooper told flight attendants that he had a bomb. He demanded $200,000 in cash and a parachute.

The plane landed in Seattle, the passengers got off, and the money and parachute were collected. With only the flight crew and D.B. Cooper on board, the plane took off again, bound for Mexico.

As the flight headed south, the hijacker put on the parachute, lowered a staircase in the back of the plane, and jumped over the rugged wilderness of the Pacific Northwest. Officially, he was never heard from again, but some of the ransom money was found in the Oregon woods, not far from Marla's grandmother's house.

It was the next day that Marla's uncle returned, saying that he had had a car accident.

"My uncle L.D. was wearing a white T-shirt and he was bloody and bruised and a mess, and I was horrified," Marla Cooper related to ABC News. "I ran inside the house and I was spying on them from around the back of my grandmother's house. And I heard my uncle say, 'We did it. Our money problems are over. We've hijacked an airplane.'"

Marla went on to say that her uncles asked her father to go into the woods to help them retrieve the money. The F.B.I. believes that the real hijacker, if he lived, lost most of the money in the deep woods of Oregon.

In a conversation Marla had with her father just before he died in 1995, they talked about her uncle, L.D. He asked if she remembered when he "hijacked that airplane," and it stirred memories of that Thanksgiving long ago.

Marla Cooper turned over to investigators a couple of items that she says belonged to her uncle, which were dusted for fingerprints. The F.B.I. will not officially comment further on the case, so the mystery continues about who D.B. Cooper really was. But not for Marla Cooper.

"I'm certain he was my uncle."

1. three phrases to start the conversation: _____

_____

2. one phrase to summarize, followed by a short summary of the article: _____

_____

3. supporting details in the article:

*What?*_____

*When?*_____

*Who?*_____

*Where?*_____

*How?*_____

_____

*Why?*_____

4. your reaction to and opinion about the facts in the article: _____

_____

_____

_____

O. A news story. Read a news story in a newspaper or online. Take notes so that you'll be able to tell your classmates about what you read. Your notes should include phrases from the **Communicative Strategies**. You can use the outline in Activity N to guide you.

TALK

P. Peer correction. Compare the conversations you wrote in Activity L to those of your classmates. Make corrections to any errors that they point out to you.

Q. World population. Talk to a classmate about the article you read in Activity M. Use phrases from the **Communicative Strategies** to start the conversation, to summarize, to answer questions about details, to react, and to give your opinion.

R. Infamous hijacker. Discuss the article about D.B. Cooper from Activity N with several classmates. Use phrases from the **Communicative Strategies** to start the conversation, to summarize the article, to answer questions about details, to react, and to give your opinion.

FBI sketch of D.B. Cooper

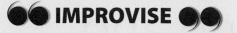

🔊🔊 **IMPROVISE** 🔊🔊

🔊 **S.** LISTENING Missing for a month. Listen to the radio news report and answer the questions **who**, **what**, **when**, **where**, **why**, and **how**.

 T. **You and the news.** Using your answers from Activity A, talk to your classmates about how, when, where, and why you find out what's going on in the world. Explain why you think or don't think that following current events is important.

U. **A news story.** Talk to a classmate about the article you read for Activity O. Use phrases to summarize, to give details, to react, and to answer questions. When you're done, your classmate will tell you about his or her article.

INTERNET RESEARCH What's new today? Read some news stories online. Select one that you find particularly interesting and tell your classmates about it. Be prepared to give your reaction to the article, to summarize it, to give the details, and to give your opinion about it. Use the phrases for talking about the news that you learned in this chapter.

5 Persuading and Responding to Objections

"But don't you see…"

Strategies for Communication

PREPARE

A. **PRE-LISTENING A worthy cause.** Read the following conversation. First, <u>underline</u> the phrases Noriko uses to persuade Kate. Next, circle (◯) the phrases Kate uses to hesitate and ask for more information. Finally, place a check (✔) on the phrases that show Kate has been persuaded.

Noriko: Hey Kate! I haven't seen you in a while. I've been meaning to call you because I wanted to ask you something.

Kate: Oh yeah? Uh … what's that?

Noriko: Well, you know my mom's a dentist, right? So she belongs to this terrific organization called Smiles International, and I'm helping her with a fundraiser. Would you consider making a contribution?

Kate: Gee, I'm a little short on money, but it sounds like a good cause. Can you tell me more about what they do?

Noriko: They set up clinics around the world for people who don't usually get to visit the dentist. All the workers are volunteers, so most of the donations go toward plane tickets for the dentists and supplies for the clinics.

Kate: I don't mean to sound suspicious, but are you sure that's true? I've heard that a lot of money for charities just pays the salaries of the people who work for them.

Noriko: I know what you mean. But you can check them out online. Only 15 percent of the money they receive goes toward administration. So you can believe that most contributions end up helping people who need it. Anyway, we'd appreciate your support, even if you can't give much.

Kate: Um … sure, OK. I think I can spare a few dollars if I know it's going somewhere good.

Noriko: It definitely is. They also teach kids how to take better care of their teeth.

Kate: OK, I'm sold. Can I give you a check?

B. LISTENING Will they or won't they? Listen to the conversations. First, place a check (✓) to show whether the first speaker is trying to persuade the second to do something or *not* to do something. Then, place a check (✓) to show if the second person is convinced or *not* convinced.

	FIRST PERSON		SECOND PERSON	
	Persuading to do something	Persuading *not* to do something	Is convinced	Is *not* convinced
1.				
2.				
3.				
4.				
5.				

C. LISTENING An offer you can't refuse. Listen to the conversation several times and provide the information requested below.

1. Write four phrases the first speaker uses to persuade his friend to do something.

You should _____   _____

_____   _____

2. Write four phrases the friend uses to show he's becoming convinced.

_____   _____

_____   _____

COMMUNICATIVE STRATEGIES: *How to Persuade People*

Sylvia: Would you consider buying this brand instead? It's supposed to be better.
Elena: Why do you say that? What do you mean by "better"?
Sylvia: Because this one is organic, all natural, healthier. It's more expensive, but I think we should try it. **Don't you think so?**
Elena: Well, I guess so.

CD 2
Tracks
2-6

CD 2
Track
7

PHRASES

Persuading Someone

… because + *reason*

Would you consider / mind …?

What would you say about / if …?

Could I (please) ask you (not) to …?

Could I talk you into …?

Can I get you to …?

Let's …

You / We (really) should / shouldn't …

Come on!

(Remember) You said that you …

You've got to believe / You can't believe (that) …

Do / Don't you see that / why …?

… don't you agree / think so?

I think that … / In my opinion, …

… You can see why I say that, right?

Responses

Why do you say that / think so?

How do you know (that)?

Why should / shouldn't I …?

Well, OK / maybe / if you say so.

Why not?

(Now) I see what you mean. / That makes sense.

I guess (so). / I guess you're right.

OK, you talked me into it.

I'm convinced. / I'm sold.

I'll do it.

Of course!

Note: See the *Speaker's Handbook* on page 157 for additional phrases.

D. Would you mind …? Complete each short dialogue with a logical phrase from the **Communicative Strategies.**

1. A: _____ call your sister-in-law tonight, so I think
   you should.

   B: I know. I will.

2. A: No, don't you see? They'll give you a refund if you return it.

   B: _____! I didn't understand before.

3. A: We should get the car's oil changed. We'll have problems later if we don't.

   B: _____. I just don't see why we should do it now.

4. A: _____ changing seats with me? I really prefer
   the aisle.

   B: Of course!

5. A: _____ play so many video games.

   B: Why not?

6. A: If you don't stop smoking now, you could have a lot of health problems later.

   B: _____. I'll quit tomorrow.

7. A: You need to buy two different pairs of shoes for this party.

   B: _____? I see no reason.

8. A: _____ coming with me to the grocery store?

   B: I guess so.

E. Don't you agree? For each situation, write a sentence to try to persuade someone.
   Then, write a follow-up statement that gives a convincing reason to support your idea.

Example: You want someone to sign a petition
   to send food aid to Africa.
   <u>Could I ask you to sign this petition</u>
   <u>to send food aid to Africa? Certain</u>
   <u>regions there have had terrible</u>
   <u>droughts and food shortages.</u>

1. You want to get a family member to do more recycling.

   _____

   _____

2. You want to persuade a friend to drink less soda.

   _____

   _____

3. You want to make a child understand that he or she should spend more
   time outdoors.

   _____

   _____

4. You want everyone to think that it's better to travel by train than by car.

_____

_____

5. You want an acquaintance to realize that it's wrong not to pay taxes.

_____

_____

F. Maybe … Use phrases from the **Communicative Strategies** to write logical responses to each of the statements you wrote in Activity E.

Example: supporting food aid to Africa
Of course! I want to help in any way I can.

1. recycling more

_____

2. drinking less soda

_____

3. spending more time outdoors

_____

4. traveling by train

_____

5. not paying taxes

_____

Language Focus: Personal Pronouns in Persuasion

When you are trying to persuade someone, the way you word your argument can be just as important as what you say. Using personal pronouns effectively can help others to see your point of view.

- Say **I believe** instead of **people think**. It shows that you personally are already convinced of a point of view.
- Say **you** to an individual to recognize that person's point of view.
  You make a very good point.
- Say **you** when pointing out past evidence that supports your argument.
  You said that we should consider this option, and I agree.
- Do not say **you** to highlight differences in opinion between yourself and others. For example, avoid:
  While you think this way, I think this is better.
- Say **we** to show agreement among a group that you are a part of.
  We are in agreement that …

G. **This is important!** Using the phrases from the **Communicative Strategies** for persuading, write a specific request for each situation, followed by a supporting statement. You will use these statements in Activity J.

> **Example:** You want someone to go somewhere with you.
> *Come on, let's go to Australia! Airfare has never been cheaper.*

1. You want someone to do something with you.

_____

_____

2. You want someone to give money to a cause you believe in.

_____

_____

3. You want someone to buy something you're selling.

_____

_____

4. You want someone to do you a big favor.

_____

_____

5. You give an opinion about something and want someone to agree with you.

_____

_____

Professional Context: Persuasion in Job Interviews

At some point in your professional life, you will likely have to go through the process of interviewing for a job. As potential employers ask you questions about your experiences and qualifications, it may be important to use persuasive language to try to convince them that you are the best person for the job. The most effective way to persuade others in a job interview is by stating an opinion, followed by a reason. For example:

I think that *I'm a great candidate* ***because*** *I have exceptional organizational skills.*

You should *consider me for the position* ***because*** *I have four years of experience as a manager.*

Note that a lot of phrases you've learned for persuading people are questions. You should not ask too many questions—particularly ones that try to persuade—until the interviewer invites you to do so at the end of the interview.

 TALK

 **H.** **Peer correction.** Compare the phrases you wrote to complete the dialogues in Activity D with those of your classmates. Make corrections to your answers if necessary.

I. **Don't you agree?** Move around the room and have conversations with your classmates about each of the topics in Activity E. Use the persuasive statements you wrote in Activity E and the responses you wrote in Activity F.

Cultural Connections: Advertising

Advertising is a form of persuasion that is used to sell products. Advertisements try to convince potential buyers that a product is useful, helpful, and even necessary for happiness.

One way that advertising persuades is to appeal to people's self-image. Ads try to convince you that you'll be better if you only buy what they're selling. How they do that depends on the culture. In the United States, for example, ads often target the cultural values of youth (looking and feeling young), independence (being free to do what you want), and control (being able to change things when you want). For that reason, ads often show people looking happy, confident, and enjoying the product being sold. If you can picture yourself in the shoes of those people, then the advertisement has done its job.

What kinds of strategies do advertisers use to persuade people where you're from? Where do you see advertisements? What kinds of images are used in those ads?

J. **This is important!** Try to convince a classmate to accept your point of view about the situations in Activity G. Use the statements and supporting reasons you wrote. When it's your turn to be persuaded, react to your partner's proposal. Ask for more information and decide what your response will be.

 **PREPARE**

LISTENING COMPREHENSION: *Stressed Words*

Listening for stressed words in a conversation can help you understand the meaning that the speaker wants to express. For example, a sentence like "You might be right" can communicate different ideas depending on which words are stressed and on the tone of voice that is used.

- ***You*** might be right. (but I'm not sure *he* is)
- You ***might*** be right. (but I doubt it)
- You might be ***right***! (and that surprises me)

By paying attention to stressed words, you'll be able to respond to people more effectively.

CD 2 🔊)))
Tracks
8-12

K. LISTENING **Which is it?** Listen for the stressed word in each incomplete statement. Then, place a check (✓) next to the ending that is most logical.

1. _____ but he has to work until 7:30.

   _____ or with Julia and Terry.

2. _____ or just his staff members?

   _____ or did you just hear about it?

3. _____ or wait until next year.

   _____ but I don't really want to.

4. _____ you can do it.

   _____ I'll do it tomorrow.

5. _____ you should call him.

   _____ he'll probably text you.

CD 2 🔊)))
Track
13

L. LISTENING **A bit confusing.** You will hear the following sentences in a conversation between two friends. Based on the stressed words you hear, match the meaning on the right to each statement on the left.

1. Julie is with Ben. _____
2. Eric was dating Sarah. _____
3. Ariel and Mark are friends. _____
4. Eric asked Ariel out at his party. _____
5. Why would he do that? _____
6. I heard that Brian kissed Sarah. _____
7. At school. _____
8. What did she say? _____
9. What do you think she said? _____
10. She doesn't know about the kiss. _____

a. Brian's
b. Ariel
c. ask Ariel out
d. not now
e. Ariel's answer
f. not dating
g. not Eric
h. Ray
i. not certain
j. not at the party

Felix:	Did you see that? This guy is amazing! I'm going to practice until I can do jumps like that.
Manuel:	OK, I'll admit, that does look pretty cool. **But** I think **it's a really bad idea** for you to try what he does.
Felix:	**How can you say that?** I've been doing skateboard jumps for a couple years.
Manuel:	**That may be, but** this is different. There's no board under you when you land.
Felix:	**So?** I'm young. I'm in good shape. How hard can it be?
Manuel:	**But you have to admit that** you should practice a long time before you try something like that.
Felix:	**Whatever.** You just wait and see.

PHRASES

Objections and Counter Objections

But …

(But) what about …?

(But) aren't you forgetting …?

That may be (true), but …

… is more important.

I know, but …

That's a good point, but …

I can see why you say that, but …

I don't agree with you (because) …

I'm not sure that's a good idea. / That's a (really) bad idea.

How can you say that?

If you (really) think about it, …

If you look at the evidence, (I think) you'll see that …

(But) on the other hand, …

Still, …

Besides, …

(But) You have to admit that …

The trouble is, …

I (just) don't feel like it / don't want to.

M. Yes, but … For each situation, write down a possible objection and a logical counter objection. Use various phrases from the **Communicative Strategies** in your responses.

Example: **Bob:**   It's your turn to do the dishes!
                 Steve: <u>I don't feel like it. I'm supposed</u>
                              <u>to meet Candace in an hour.</u>
                 Bob: <u>Aren't you forgetting that your</u>
                            <u>parents are coming by at 5:00?</u>

1. **Bill:** Jorge, you should spend less money eating out.

   Jorge: _____

   Bill: _____

2. **Mark:** Come on, it's not such a big deal to text during class.

   Janie: _____

   Mark: _____

3. **Mohammed:** Theresa, could I borrow your car tomorrow?

   Theresa: _____

   Mohammed: _____

4. **Carla:** I think it's possible that there's life on other planets.

   Tom: _____

   Carla: _____

5. **Suzanne:** I really like that candidate. I don't think it really matters that she has no experience.

   Tomas: _____

   Suzanne: _____

Language Focus: Double Negatives

In English, you can form negative sentences with **not** or other negative words.

• **not / -n't**	He **does not / doesn't** agree with me.
• **no**	She has **no** money.
nothing	He has **nothing** on him.
never	They **never** agree on anything.
nowhere	We're going **nowhere** tonight.

Generally speaking, you should not use more than one negative in a sentence, especially with the word **not**. To avoid double negatives, you need to use affirmative words.

• **any**	She does**n't** have **any** money.
anything	He does**n't** have **anything** on him.
ever	They do**n't ever** agree on anything.
anywhere	We're **not** going **anywhere** tonight.

You should avoid double negatives even in casual conversations.

Incorrect: I **don't** believe **nothing** she says.
Correct: I **don't** believe **anything** she says.

N. **School all year?** Read the following proposal. Then, write at least four arguments in favor of and four arguments against it, using phrases from the **Communicative Strategies**. You will use these ideas in a conversation in Activity Q. Be prepared to argue either side of the question.

Proposal: Students should be in school all year and not get a long summer vacation.

Arguments in Favor

1. _____
   _____
2. _____
   _____
3. _____
   _____
4. _____
   _____

Arguments Against

1. _____
   _____
2. _____
   _____
3. _____
   _____
4. _____
   _____

O. Peer correction. Compare the objections and counter objections you wrote in Activity M with those of your classmates. Which statements seem the most persuasive?

P. Let's agree to disagree. With a classmate, role-play the situations on the conversation cards your instructor gives you. Use words and expressions to persuade, object, counter objections, and agree to disagree. The person with Card A will begin each conversation.

Q. School all year? Have a debate with a classmate about the proposal from Activity N. Take opposite sides of the issue of year-round school, and use the arguments you wrote down to try to persuade your classmate. At the end of the conversation, decide if you are convinced of your classmate's argument or if you should agree to disagree.

R. Let's do something this weekend. Try to persuade your classmates to spend Saturday and Sunday doing several different activities, such as going to a movie, a sporting event, a museum, a concert, a restaurant, the mall, and so on. They'll propose some other ideas or object to your ideas. If they do object, counter their objections. Use phrases from the **Communicative Strategies**.

 **IMPROVISE**

CD 2
Track
14 **S.** LISTENING **Are you sure about that?** Listen to a conversation between a mother and her son as they work through a disagreement. Then, answer the questions that follow.

> **1.** What phrases does Jonathan's mother use to object to Jonathan's plan to buy a leather jacket? What reasons does she give?
>
> **2.** What phrases does Jonathan use to counter his mother's objections about the jacket? What do you think about his reasons for wanting to buy it?
>
> **3.** What language does the mother use to end their argument? Why does she end it?
>
> **4.** Do Jonathan and his mother get along? How do you know?
>
> **5.** Do you think Jonathan considers himself an adult? Explain your answer.

T. **You know I'm right!** Your instructor will give you Activity Cards. Try to persuade a classmate to agree with what's indicated on the card. Your classmate should object at first, but see whether you can change his or her mind.

U. **The American Dream.** As a class, discuss the following questions. Use the **Communicative Strategies** you've learned for making persuasive statements, raising and countering objections, and saying whether or not you're convinced.

What do you think people mean when they use the phrase "the American Dream"? What are examples of this dream? What about American society makes it possible? What obstacles can make it hard to succeed? What specific examples can you think of where people have lived the American Dream?

 INTERNET RESEARCH Advertising techniques. Find some advertisements online. Make a note of what images and words the ads use to try to persuade people to buy their product, take some action, and so on. Present one ad to your class. Talk about the persuasive techniques that the ad uses.

6 Talking about the Visual Arts

"What do you like about it?"

 **PREPARE**

A. PRE-LISTENING **What do you see?** For each image, write down (a) the type of art it is (painting, tattoo, graffiti), (b) what you see in it (content, shapes, colors), and (c) what it makes you think of. You'll discuss these pieces of art with your classmates.

1.

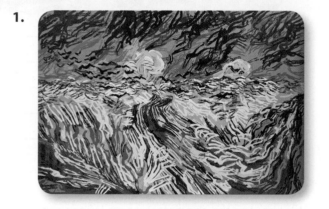

a. Type of art: _____

b. Description: _____

_____

c. Reaction: _____

_____

2.

a. Type of art: _____

b. Description: _____

_____

c. Reaction: _____

_____

3.

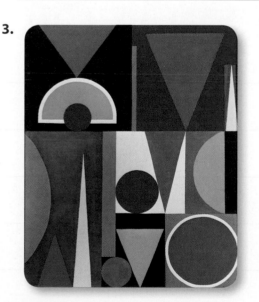

a. Type of art: _____

b. Description: _____

_____

c. Reaction: _____

_____

4.

a. Type of art: _____

b. Description: _____

_____

c. Reaction: _____

_____

5.

a. Type of art: _____

b. Description: _____
_____

c. Reaction: _____
_____

6.

a. Type of art: _____

b. Description: _____
_____

c. Reaction: _____
_____

CD 2
Tracks
15–20

B. LISTENING **What type of art is it?** Listen to the short statements. Write the type of art that people are describing.

> **Types of art:**
> painting / photograph / jewelry / architecture / tattoo / stained glass / graffiti / cave art / statue

1. _____

2. _____

3. _____

4. _____

5. _____

6. _____

C. LISTENING Van Gogh's bedroom. Listen to the conversation. Write down the words and phrases you hear that describe the painting.

Vincent van Gogh, *Bedroom at Arles*, 1889

_____

_____

_____

_____

_____

_____

COMMUNICATIVE STRATEGIES: *How to Describe a Work of Art*

Vincent van Gogh, *The Starry Night*, 1889

Simon: *Starry Night* always makes me a bit **uneasy**.

Elise: Why? It gives me the opposite **impression**. The stars, the moon, the peaceful small town with the church as the center point, the large dark tree in the foreground, the lights in the windows …

Simon: To me, van Gogh **is showing** how big nature is and how small humans are. The town's buildings are tiny compared to the huge clouds and the large stars. And that's not a tree … it's a large, dark mountain, **I think**. And it dominates the **foreground**. And the whole thing is so dark! **It reminds me** of when I was a kid and just terrified of the dark. Maybe that's why I feel that way about this painting.

Elise: Could be. But I think it also shows what a genius van Gogh was. Each person who looks at *Starry Night* has a different **reaction** to it. It's a **masterpiece**.

PHRASES

General Impression
Adjectives

abstract	colorful	fascinating	impressive	realistic
beautiful	confusing	fun	interesting	sad
calm	dark	funny	overwhelming	scary
chaotic	disturbing	happy	peaceful	violent

Phrases

It reminds me of …
It gives me the impression …
It makes me think of …
It makes me uneasy / nervous / happy / sad / *etc.*
It's a masterpiece.

Subject

The painting / photograph / mural / watercolor / tapestry / graffiti / tattoo / *etc.* …
… portrays / shows / represents / depicts …
In the picture, you can see …
It's an image of …
It's a scene of …
It's about …

Composition (directional words)

In the foreground / background …
In the upper / lower part …
In the upper / lower left-hand / right-hand corner …
In front of / behind / next to / above / below / across from / near / between …
On the right / left (side) …
In the middle / center …
In the distance, you can just (barely) make out / see the outline of …
The focal point is …
The point that draws your attention is …

Shapes and Colors
Shapes

circles / triangles / squares / ovals / rectangles
exaggerated / odd / unnatural … shapes

Colors

primary colors: red / yellow / blue
bright / light / dark / vivid / bold / subdued / pale / warm / hot / cool / cold … colors

Interpreting Art

I think / believe that (the artist) …
It seems to me that (the artist) …
The painter is trying to show …
The artist seems to be trying to capture …
The photographer is criticizing …
The sculptor wants to show …

Note: See the *Speaker's Handbook* on page 157 for additional phrases.

D. Two villages. Write down words and phrases from the **Communicative Strategies** to describe the paintings of two different villages.

_____

_____

_____

_____

_____

_____

E. A personal photograph. Select a photo from your personal collection and write down phrases to describe it. What's the subject? Who's in it? What's the scene? When was it taken? What memories does it bring to you? Is this photo important to you or someone you know? Why? If possible, bring the photo to class so that you can show it to your classmates as you describe it.

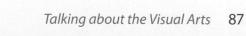

When you describe the colors of an object (such as a painting, a house, a car, lipstick, clothing, a bicycle, flowers, hair, eyes, etc.), you can help someone visualize it better if you are specific about the color. For example, is something **dark red** or **bright red**? Is it a **blue green** or more of a **yellow green**? Is it an **off white** or a **pure (bright) white**? Is it a **light shade of purple**? Is it **blue black** or **jet black**? Is it **a mixture of red and orange**? Is it **more pink than red**? Is it **more of a yellow rather than an orange**?

F. **A work of art.** Look at any work of art in a book, online, or in a museum. Use as many words and phrases from the **Communicative Strategies** as you can to describe it (subject, structure, shapes, colors, interpretations).

Name of the artist (if known): _____

Name of the work of art: _____

Description: _____

_____

_____

_____

_____

_____

_____

_____

G. What do you see? Discuss the works of art from Activity A with your classmates. In your conversation, use the notes you made and words and phrases from the **Communicative Strategies**. How are your classmates' reactions to the pieces of art different from yours?

H. Two villages. Talk about the two paintings in Activity D with a classmate. Compare your descriptions and your reactions to each painting.

I. A personal photograph. Describe the photo you selected in Activity E to a classmate. Your classmate can ask you questions for clarification and additional information.

J. A work of art. Tell your classmates about the work of art you selected in Activity F. Be sure to talk about subject, composition, shapes, colors, and how you interpret it. Your classmates can ask you questions for clarification and additional information.

K. Carmen Lomas Garza (b. 1948). Work with your classmates. Use the phrases you learned in the **Communicative Strategies** to discuss this painting by the Mexican-American artist Carmen Lomas Garza.

Carmen Lomas Garza, *La Feria en Reynosa (the Fair in Reynosa)*, 1987

Part Two

 PREPARE ●●

LISTENING COMPREHENSION: *Word Families*

Word families are groups of words that look and sound similar and are based on similar meanings. For example:

paint	**art**	**history**
painter	**artist**	**historian**
painting	**artistic**	**historical**

If you're not sure of a word you hear, you might know a word of the same family that will help you understand the general meaning of the word. For example:

- you hear the adjective **chaotic**
- you know the noun **chaos**
- you understand that **chaotic** means "a lot of chaos"

Connecting words by families not only expands your vocabulary but also can make it easier to understand what others say.

CD 2
Track
22

L. LISTENING **Word connections.** Listen carefully to each word and write down a word that you know from the same word family.

Example: You hear: *miraculous*
You write: **miracle**

1. _____

2. _____

3. _____

4. _____

5. _____

6. _____

7. _____

8. _____

9. _____

10. _____

M. **LISTENING** **Words of the same family.** Listen to the conversation and write down any words you hear for which you can come up with other words in the same family. Write the words below.

Example: You hear: *tonight* Words in the same family: **night, nightly,** etc.

Words from the conversation	Words in the same family
_____	_____
_____	_____
_____	_____
_____	_____
_____	_____
_____	_____
_____	_____
_____	_____
_____	_____

Cultural Connections: Watching Movies

Watching movies is a significant part of American culture. This is partly due to the fact that so many movies are produced in the United States, and also because there are so many ways to watch movies.

Going to the movies at a theater is usually a popular social event among friends and family. It most frequently happens on Fridays and Saturdays, usually after having dinner at a restaurant. Another part of the American movie-going experience is visiting the "concession stand" in the theater lobby to buy movie snacks like popcorn, candy, nachos, and soda.

It has become easier for people to watch movies at home, too. Large home entertainment systems can give you the feel of being in a movie theater. Family and friends can watch movies on DVDs (digital video discs), movies on-demand (through a TV cable subscription service), movies recorded with a DVR (digital video recorder), and movies streaming on the Internet.

Many families have a regular "movie night" at home, usually on weekends. Parents and children make popcorn, pick a movie to watch, and spend the evening together. These events can also include friends and neighbors.

What ways do people watch movies where you're from? Is watching movies a social event that includes a lot of people? Where do you watch movies (at home, in theaters, in other public places)?

COMMUNICATIVE STRATEGIES: *How to Talk about a Movie*

Joshua: Hey Sang-hee, have you seen the movie *True Grit*? It's not new. It came out in 2010 …

Sang-hee: No, I don't know it. *Grit*? What does that word mean?

Joshua: Well in this case, *grit* refers to someone who has a "strong character and courage." Anyway, **the movie is about** a 14-year-old girl from Arkansas in the 1800s who has the grit to find the killer of her father. Hailee Steinfeld **plays** the **main character** Mattie Ross. And Jeff Bridges and Matt Damon play the men who help her.

Sang-hee: So how do you know the story?

Joshua: Well, actually I read the book. I haven't seen the movie, but **I hear it's supposed to be really good.** The acting got great reviews.

Sang-hee: So it's a **western**?

Joshua: Um … yes, that's the **setting**, but the **message** is about justice and friendship. So you wanna go with me? It's playing tonight at the student union.

Sang-hee: Sure. I'd like that.

PHRASES

Watching the Movies

to go to the movies
to watch a movie (on TV)
to watch a DVD
name of movie + is playing at + *name of movie theater*
there's a show at + *time*

Types of Movies

action-adventure	disaster movie	horror	romantic (comedy)
animated	documentary	love story	science fiction
biography	drama	musical (comedy)	spy movie
comedy	fantasy	mystery	thriller
crime drama	historical drama	psychological thriller	western

Characteristics of a Movie

3D (three-dimensional)	dialogue	plot	subtitles
acting	dubbed (dialogue)	scene	suspense
action	foreign movie	setting	title
the beginning / ending	a hit / blockbuster / box-office smash	soundtrack [music] special effects	violence

People Involved in Movies

actor	(main / supporting) characters	good guy / hero	screenwriter
actress		producer	(movie) star
bad guy / villain	director		

About the Movies

I just saw … / I want to go see … / I haven't seen …

I like / love / don't like / hate this movie.

I liked / loved / didn't like / hated …

What do / did you think of …

I thought it was terrible / great / wonderful / scary / disappointing / well done / good / bad / depressing / bizarre / sad / interesting / sensational / *etc.*

(I heard) It's supposed to be + *adjective*

The movie is about …

What kind of movie is it?

Who's in it? / Who's starring in it? / Who are the actors?

What does the title mean?

What's the message of this movie?

Note: See the *Speaker's Handbook* on page 157 for additional phrases.

N. **Words of the same family.** Review the words and phrases in the **Communicative Strategies**. Make a list of the words for which you can come up with other words in the same family.

Example: *adventure* **adventurer**

O. You and the movies. Answer the following questions to prepare for conversations you'll have in class. For each answer, include words and expressions from the **Communicative Strategies**.

1. How often do you watch movies? Where? With whom? _____
_____
_____

2. Name four or five *types* of movies you especially like. _____
_____
_____

3. Name four or five *types* of movies you really dislike. _____
_____
_____

4. In your opinion, of all the people involved in making movies, who are the most important? Why? _____
_____
_____

5. What characteristics of movies are you most interested in? Why? _____
_____
_____

6. What is the last movie you saw? Did you like it? Why or why not? _____
_____
_____
_____
_____

Language Focus: Etiquette for Discussing Movies

After you've seen a movie, you might be tempted to talk about it with people. Before you get into too many details about the movie, consider that others who haven't seen it may want to eventually. Here are some things you should remember when talking about a movie.

- Ask people if they've already seen the movie or if they plan to.
- Don't give away the ending unless people invite you to do so.
- Whether you liked the movie or not, give only general opinions about it. ("I liked the story." "I'm not crazy about fantasy.") You don't want to give away too many details if you liked it, nor discourage others from seeing it if you didn't.
- Be aware of people who may overhear your comments about a movie, especially when you're leaving the theater, so that you don't spoil it for others.
- Don't act like an expert movie critic. Give others a chance to share their opinions.
- Talk about a movie's strengths and weaknesses.
- As with any other visual art, your reactions to movies are a matter of personal opinion, and it's important to think about the people around you before you share it.

TALK

P. **Peer correction.** Compare the word list you made in Activity N with those of your classmates. Write down any words you don't have.

Q. **You and the movies.** Move around the room and use your answers from Activity O to talk to several classmates about your movie-watching habits. Use proper etiquette when you talk about the movies you've seen. If a classmate has not seen the movie you want to talk about, move on to someone else.

R. **A favorite flick.** Talk to a classmate about one of your favorite movies. Before you begin, ask your classmate if he or she has seen the movie and if you can tell its story. If so, talk about the story, the actors, what you liked, and why you liked it. Use phrases from the **Communicative Strategies**.

Professional Context: Movies as Big Business

The movie industry is big business in the U.S. Billions of dollars are spent to produce movies and billions of dollars are earned in ticket sales and merchandise. According to the Motion Picture Association of America, over 2 million people work in the television and movie industries in the U.S.

A movie does not have to receive favorable reviews by critics to make a lot of money. Moviegoers are drawn more to a movie's action, visual images, and special effects than to its plot and acting. Much of the financial success of a movie depends on how interested viewers are to experience it on a big screen in a theater.

In the last 35 years, the movie industry has grown significantly. Here are the box office earnings at the beginning of each decade:

- 1980 - $2.75 billion
- 1990 - $5 billion
- 2000 - $7.7 billion
- 2010 - $10.6 billion

IMPROVISE

CD 2
Track
24

S. **LISTENING** *True Grit.* Listen to a radio DJ talk about the movie *True Grit*. Then, discuss the questions with a small group.

True Grit	
1968:	Novel by Charles Portis
1969:	Original film adaptation, with John Wayne as Rooster Cogburn
2010:	New film adaptation by the Coen brothers
Cast:	Jeff Bridges (Rooster Cogburn); Hailee Steinfeld (Mattie Ross); Josh Brolin (Tom Chaney); Matt Damon (LaBoeuf)

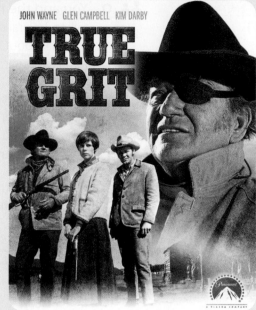

1. Who narrates the story in *True Grit*? When?

2. How old was Mattie when her adventures began?

3. What kind of a girl was she?

4. What's the reason for her adventure?

5. Who are the people who help her?

6. What is Rooster Cogburn like?

7. What are some of the things that happen to Mattie along the way?

8. What are some of the themes of *True Grit*?

T. **What I see.** Take some time to look at the three paintings. Then, tell your classmates which one of the three you prefer and why. Talk about subject, shapes, colors, and the artists' intentions.

 U. The visual arts. Have a conversation with your classmates about the visual arts. Talk about why you do or do not think that art is important. Discuss questions about the arts. Should people visit museums? Should students study art in school? Should artists receive money from organizations to support their work? If you like to draw, paint, take pictures, or make movies, talk about your experiences and what it does for you.

INTERNET RESEARCH Classic movies. Go online and find information about a movie that's considered a classic. Write some notes about it. Who was the director? Who were the actors? What's the basic plot? Why do you think it's considered a classic? Use the phrases you learned to tell your classmates about the movie you chose. If possible, watch the movie.

Possible movies:
Casablanca, Psycho, The African Queen, Citizen Kane, Easy Rider, E.T.: The Extra-Terrestrial, Fantasia, The Godfather, Gone with the Wind, King Kong, North by Northwest, Notorious, One Flew Over the Cuckoo's Nest, Star Wars, To Kill a Mockingbird, 2001: A Space Odyssey, West Side Story, The Wizard of Oz, The Jazz Singer

7 Resolving Conflicts

"We can work this out."

Strategies for Communication

Part 1: How to Discuss a Problem

Part 2: How to Express a Willingness to Compromise

●● PREPARE ●●

A. PRE-LISTENING **I can't believe this!** Read the phone conversation.

- <u>Underline</u> the phrases Judy uses to introduce and comment on her problems. ("Well, first …," "It was a real nightmare," etc.)
- Circle ◯ the phrases her friend Mario uses to react to Judy's problems and to encourage her to keep talking about them.

Mario: Hey, good to hear from you! How's your trip going? Start at the beginning. Like, how was your flight?

Judy: Well, it was pretty awful, actually.

Mario: Why? What happened?

Judy: There was this storm that shook the plane. Everyone around me got sick.

Mario: That's terrible. Well, at least you made it there. Is your hotel OK?

Judy: Yeah, it's fine, but that was the next big mess. Apparently there are *two* hotels called Excelsior here, and my taxi took me to the wrong one. I was exhausted, and it took me another hour to get into my room in the right hotel.

Mario: You're kidding! I'm so sorry. I hope everything's been better since then.

Judy: Ha, oh no, there's more. It's much colder than I expected it to be, and I'm *freezing*.

Mario: I guess you're going to have to go shopping.

Judy: I know. That's not such a big deal, I guess. I just wish I had been prepared.

Mario: You're still meeting up with your cousins, aren't you?

Judy: Well, to top it off, it turns out that Francine couldn't come after all.

Mario: No! So what are you gonna do?

Judy: Oh, Claudine is still coming, and the two of us will have fun together. And actually, that solves another problem. I was only able to get two concert tickets. I didn't know what we were going to do for the third person, but since Francine isn't coming, that takes care of it.

Mario: Well, that's good, anyway. Maybe your luck is improving!

CD 2
Tracks
25-30

B. **LISTENING** **What's the problem?** Write the letter of the image that goes with each of the short conversations.

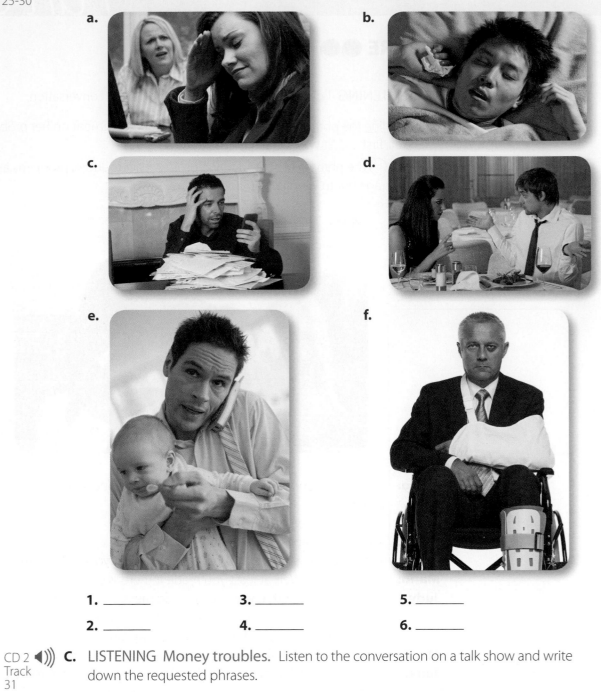

a.

b.

c.

d.

e.

f.

1. _____   **3.** _____   **5.** _____

2. _____   **4.** _____   **6.** _____

CD 2
Track
31

C. **LISTENING** **Money troubles.** Listen to the conversation on a talk show and write down the requested phrases.

1. General phrases Sean and Sally (the hostess) use to indicate a problem: _____

_____

2. Phrases Sean uses to ask for help or advice: _____

_____

3. Phrases Brad uses to ask for information and to show he wants to help: _____

_____

4. Phrases Brad uses to give advice to Sean: _____

_____

Mark: Hey, it's Mark. I think **I have a problem**. Could you come over?
Neighbor: **What's wrong?**
Mark: I think someone is trying to break into the house!
Neighbor: **Don't worry** and **stay** calm. It's probably just an animal.
Mark: **But that's not all**. The outside lights aren't working and my back door is unlocked.
Neighbor: I think I better call the police. In the meantime, **turn on** all your indoor lights and **lock** the doors.
Mark: Thanks, Mr. Wilson.

PHRASES

Raising a Problem

I've / We've got a (little / bit of a / real) problem (on my hands / on our hands)!

I can't believe this (is happening)!

What a mess! / This is a (real / big) mess / nightmare!

I'm in (a little) trouble.

Reacting

What's wrong? / What's the matter? / What is it? / What's going on?

What happened? (Who? / What? / When? / Where? / Why? / How?)

Tell me (about it)!

Expressing Concern

Oh no!

That's too bad! / That's not good.

That's / This is terrible / unbelievable!

You're kidding!

Don't worry!

Guess this just isn't your day …

You just can't catch a break …

I hope it all works out.

Bringing Up Further Complications

And to make matters worse …

And as if things weren't bad enough (already) …

But that's not all! / But wait, there's more!

To add insult to injury …

And to top it all off …

Asking for Advice

I don't know what to do.

What do you think I should do?

What should I / we do (about it)?

Proposing a Solution

(Maybe) + *personal pronoun* + can / could / should …

You should probably …

We can / need to figure this out.

How can I help? / Maybe I / we can help.

Commands: Ask for help. / Don't give up. / *etc.*

Note: See the *Speaker's Handbook* on page 157 for additional phrases.

D. Tell me. Put the sentences of each short conversation in their correct order by writing the corresponding letter next to the speaker.

1. Rosie: _____

    Teresa: _____

    Rosie: _____

    Teresa: _____

    Rosie: _____

a. But that's not all! I returned all the books to the library yesterday!

b. What's wrong?

c. Uh-oh, that's not good.

d. Hey Teresa. I'm in a little trouble.

e. I finished my term paper, but I forgot to include a bibliography, and it's due in an hour.

2. Luke: _____

    Scott: _____

    Luke: _____

    Scott: _____

    Luke: _____

    Scott: _____

a. It must have been last night after I got home from work.

b. Ah, I can't believe this is happening! Somebody hit my car and didn't leave a note.

c. That's unbelievable! I didn't hear anything. Do you know when?

d. Just right outside our apartment here on the street.

e. Really? Where?

f. Wow, you just can't catch a break.

3. Allie: _____

    Tarik: _____

    Allie: _____

    Tarik: _____

    Allie: _____

    Tarik: _____

    Allie: _____

a. I don't know. But that's not all. He's been suspended for the rest of the week. What are we gonna do about this?

b. We've got a little problem on our hands.

c. Maybe we should call the principal.

d. We do? Tell me about it.

e. Aidan was sent home from school today for fighting.

f. Don't call yet. We need to figure out what happened with Aidan first.

g. That's terrible! What happened?

E. What's the problem? Read the reactions to problems in these short dialogues. Using phrases from the **Communicative Strategies**, write a logical statement that raises the problem to complete each exchange.

Example: _I've got a little problem. I think my cousin stole some money from me._
          That's too bad! Are you going to ask him about it?

1. _____

Don't worry! You've got two full days to finish it.

2. _____

That's unbelievable! Have you called the police?

3. _____

That's not good. You should probably stay home and rest.

4. _____

I don't know. But maybe we can talk to her supervisor.

5. _____

That's too bad. Guess this just isn't your day.

6. _____

What happened? Tell me about it!

F. **Common problems.** Think about the four topics below, which commonly cause problems for people. Then, invent four specific problems about each of these topics. Write down a few phrases you might use to introduce these problems to others. You will use this information with your classmates to discuss problems in Activity H.

> **Topics:**
>
> family / money / school / work

Invented problems:

1. _____

_____

_____

2. _____

_____

_____

3. _____

_____

_____

4. _____

_____

_____

Phrases to discuss the problems: _____

_____

_____

_____

_____

●● TALK ●●

G. Peer correction. Compare the sentences you wrote in Activity E with those of your classmates. Write down any of their statements for introducing problems that are particularly creative.

H. Common problems. Move around the room and role-play discussions about the problems you wrote down in Activity F with four different classmates. Use the phrases you wrote down to introduce the problems. Your classmates will react and ask you follow-up questions. When finished with one topic, switch roles and discuss another problem before moving on to the next person.

I. Maybe you could … Your instructor will give you a situation card that explains a problem you have, along with a complication that makes the situation worse. Raise the problem with a classmate. He or she will react, ask follow-up questions, and propose some solutions. Invent answers to your classmate's questions and responses to any solutions.

Cultural Connections: Speaking Out Against Bullying

Bullying—the threat or the act of violence against another person—is not a new problem in the United States. But because more people are raising the issue now than in the past, it is receiving national attention as a problem that needs a solution.

Traditionally, bullying has happened most often in schools. But with advances in communication technology, a new form of bullying has emerged that is even harder to stop because it is everywhere: **cyberbullying**. Through texts, chats, e-mails, and postings on blogs and social media websites, it is easier for bullies to embarrass or threaten others—and now without even having to face the victims in person. An Associated Press–MTV poll from 2011 revealed that 56 percent of people in their teens and twenties had been targeted by cyberbullies.

Almost all 50 states have some sort of law against bullying, but there is no federal law against cyberbullying. (State laws *can* be interpreted to include cyberbullying in most cases.) Anyone who feels that he or she is being intimidated by a bully—either in person or online—should report the problem immediately to someone in authority.

Is bullying a problem where you're from? Is cyberbullying? If so, what kinds of solutions are there to help deal with these problems?

PREPARE

LISTENING COMPREHENSION: *Time Words*

Time words are the words people use to indicate when events happen in relation to other events. Listening for time words can help you understand the order that things happen in situations with a lot of details.

Many time words fall into two categories:

1. Words that relate to a particular moment: **today**, **yesterday**, **tomorrow**, **now**, **next week**, **last year**, **this month**, **minutes ago**, **hours ago**, **that morning**, **this evening**, **at** *(time)* **o'clock**, **soon**, **a long time ago**, and so on.

   > Your papers are due **at 10:00 Thursday morning**. No extensions!
   > I'm getting a raise **this month**, but I won't be promoted until **next year**.
   > They left **three hours ago**. I'm sure they'll call **soon**.

2. Words that relate events to each other: **afterwards**, **after (that)**, **as soon as**, **then**, **before**, **already**, **later**, **first**, **next**, **last**, **finally**, **to begin with**, **at the same moment**, **at the same time**, **meanwhile**, **since**, **while**, and so on.

   > We'll leave **as soon as** she gets here.
   > I **already** took out the trash! Stop asking!
   > You should never drive and text **at the same time**.

CD 2  **J.** LISTENING **A matter of time.** Listen to short exchanges from several conversations.
Tracks   First, identify the time words that you hear and write them down. Then, listen again and
32-35   put the events in order (1, 2, 3, etc.), using the time words to help you.

1. Time words: _____

   _____ boy invites girl to go camping   _____ girl says she can't go

   _____ boy comes to pick girl up

2. Time words: _____

   _____ boy believes he has to take a   _____ boy and girl laugh about
             friend to the hospital   the situation

   _____ boy studies really hard   _____ girl panics

3. Time words: _____

   _____ man honks his horn   _____ man sees other car backing up

   _____ man gets hit by other car   _____ man is stopped at a traffic light

   _____ driver of other car is talking on cell phone

4. Time words: _____

   _____ woman cleans out purse   _____ son puts on jeans

   _____ woman buys jeans for son   _____ woman returns to the store

   _____ woman tells husband son is taller   _____ son grows two inches

K. LISTENING Once upon a knight. Listen to the fairy tale. The first time you listen, write down any time words you hear in the story. Then, listen again for the events below that are listed in pairs. Finally, write one sentence that shows the relationship between the two events using one of the time words you wrote down.

Example: **Event 1:** The knight arrives at the castle.
Event 2: The knight is attacked and his horse stolen.
Sentence: <u>Sir Rowan was attacked and his horse was stolen the week</u>
<u>before he arrived at the castle.</u>

Time words: <u>the week before,</u> _____

_____

1. **Event 1:** The knight crosses the border into the king's lands.

   Event 2: The knight walks without a horse.

   Sentence: _____

   _____

2. **Event 1:** The royal doctor bandages the knight's wounds.

   Event 2: The knight enters the castle.

   Sentence: _____

   _____

3. **Event 1:** The court minister enters the room.

   Event 2: The princess is going to tell her father that she wants to become a knight.

   Sentence: _____

   _____

4. **Event 1:** The knight is eating supper.

   Event 2: The princess asks the knight questions about his adventures.

   Sentence: _____

   _____

5. **Event 1:** Sir Rowan tells the princess that being a knight is terrible.

   Event 2: The princess tells Sir Rowan that it is her dream to be a knight.

   Sentence: _____

   _____

6. **Event 1:** The princess secretly learns the skills to be a knight.

   Event 2: The king doesn't know what the princess is doing.

   Sentence: _____

   _____

7. Event 1: The king orders all knights to destroy the Dragon Grimm.

Event 2: The Dragon Grimm terrorizes the kingdom.

Sentence: _____

_____

8. Event 1: The princess leaves the castle.

Event 2: The princess asks the knight what he wants in return.

Sentence: _____

_____

9. Event 1: A mysterious figure appears at the castle door.

Event 2: The princess travels to the land of Grimm.

Sentence: _____

_____

10. Event 1: The crowd noise dies down.

Event 2: The king says, "You have served your kingdom well."

Sentence: _____

_____

11. Event 1: The princess says, "Thank you, father."

Event 2: The princess removes her helmet.

Sentence: _____

_____

12. Event 1: The princess stands and the king hugs her.

Event 2: The king calls his daughter a knight.

Sentence: _____

_____

Language Focus: Exclamations

When talking about problems, people often use exclamations to express themselves emotionally. Some words can turn declarative statements into exclamations.

Exclamations with nouns are often expressed with **What a …!, such a …!,** or **so many …!**

That was a disaster.	**What a** disaster that was!
She had a hard time.	She had **such a** hard time!
Things went wrong.	**So many** things went wrong!

Exclamations with adjectives or adverbs often include the words **really** or **so**.

He was hurt **so** badly!	That's a **really** bad idea!

Note: Sometimes, **how** is also used with adjectives in exclamations.

How odd! Did he really say that?	**How** scary! Did you call the police?

Maryann:	**OK, so here's the problem.** I want to paint our building red, but you prefer it to be gold.
Frank:	I do *not* want my house to be red. **So what are we going to do about it?**
Maryann:	Well, I think that shade of gold is really ugly. **There must be some way to resolve this.**
Frank:	**Maybe we could** choose a different color that both of us like.
Maryann:	I don't know. We don't agree on much. **How about this?** You paint your side gold, and I'll paint my side red.
Frank:	**I guess** we could try it. We'll see how it looks.

PHRASES

Summarizing the Problem

So, you (don't) want / need …

… and I can't / (don't) want / need …

To sum up, …

So, here's where we are / stand.

So, these are the things we haven't agreed on yet.

As I see it, this is the problem.

OK, so here's the problem.

Calling for a Resolution

So, what can we do (about this)?

What are we going to do?

How can we sort this out?

How are we going to resolve this?

We need to find a solution.

There must be some way to resolve this.

I'm sure we can think of something.

How should we settle this?

Suggesting a Compromise

Can we come to an agreement / find a way to compromise?

Could we meet halfway / in the middle?

We can make this work if we …

We can work this out.

(How about this?) If you …, then I …

Maybe you / I could …

I'd be willing to …

Coming to an Agreement

OK, I can live with that.

OK, that works (for me).

I guess that's OK.

Great idea! I knew we'd find a solution.

Note: See the *Speaker's Handbook* on page 157 for additional phrases.

L. **We can work this out.** Read each situation and problem between two people. Then, complete their conversation in which they try to reach a compromise. Follow the prompts in parentheses and use phrases from the **Communicative Strategies**.

1. *Situation:* Cindy and Samir have tickets to go to a concert in the city.

Problem: Cindy wants to take public transportation. Samir wants to rent a car.

Cindy *(summarizes the problem):* _____

_____

Samir *(calls for a resolution):* _____

_____

Cindy *(suggests a compromise):* _____

_____

Samir *(comes to an agreement):* _____

_____

2. *Situation:* There is a party at the neighbor's house Friday, which is tonight.

Problem: The wife wants to go to the party. The husband doesn't want to go out.

Wife *(summarizes the problem):* _____

_____

Husband *(calls for a resolution):* _____

_____

Wife *(suggests a compromise):* _____

_____

Husband *(comes to an agreement):* _____

_____

M. I have a suggestion. Look at the images and read the captions. For each problem, write a possible compromise that someone might suggest. Use the phrases from the **Communicative Strategies**.

Example: Who's paying the check?

<u>How about this? If you let me pay the</u>
<u>check, you can leave the tip.</u>

1.

I would really like this last piece of pie.

_____

_____

_____

2.

Who's going to clean up this mess?

_____

_____

_____

3.

That's really expensive! Any chance you could lower the price?

_____

_____

_____

4.

I know, I know. It's almost dinner.

_____

_____

_____

5.  Can we keep him, please?

_____

_____

_____

N. What should we do about this? For each pair of people listed, invent a problem that might arise between them. Then, write two sentences that one of them might say to summarize the problem and call for a resolution.

Example: an employee and a manager
As I see it, this is the problem: I really need you to come in this weekend, but you have family in town. How can we work this out?

1. two neighbors

_____

_____

2. two roommates or housemates

_____

_____

3. a salesperson and a customer

_____

_____

4. two coworkers

_____

_____

Professional Context: Resolving Conflicts in the Workplace

In most workplaces in the United States, there are procedures in place to help coworkers resolve problems or conflicts.

- First, you are expected to talk to the person with whom you're having the problem and try to work out your differences.
- If that doesn't work, you can then go to a manager or supervisor.
- If the problem still isn't resolved, you can go to the Human Resources department or request a mediator—a third party who tries to resolve the conflict objectively.

In most cases, the two coworkers can usually resolve conflicts without involving anyone else. It is considered the adult and professional way to deal with interpersonal problems. But some situations do require more help.

●● TALK ●●

O. Peer correction. Compare your answers in Activity M to those of your classmates. Write down any phrases for resolving problems that you find useful.

P. I have a suggestion. Compare the compromises that you and your classmates came up with in Activity N. Which compromises do you feel would work best in each situation?

Q. What should we do about this? Using the problems you came up with in Activity N, start a conversation with a classmate in which each of you plays a role. Summarize the problem for him or her and call for a resolution. Then, improvise the rest of the conversation until you've reached a compromise. Use phrases from the **Communicative Strategies**. When finished, listen to your classmate summarize a different problem and call for a resolution.

Example: an employee and a boss
  A: *As I see it, this is the problem: I really need you to come in this weekend, but you have family in town. How can we work this out?*
  B: *Well, I haven't seen my cousins in so long. Is there any chance you could get someone else to come in?*
  A: *How about this? If you give me your cell phone number, you can stay home with your cousins, and I can call you only if we have questions. Would that work?*
  B: *Yes, I can definitely live with that. And thanks for understanding.*

R. Maybe we could … You and your classmates play the roles of people who live together (family, roommates, etc.). At least one of you is not at all concerned with conserving water or electricity, or recycling paper and plastic. At least one of you is passionate about the environment. Work out a compromise that everyone in the house can live with.

🗨️ IMPROVISE 🗨️

CD 2 🔊
Track
37

S. **LISTENING** It's a lot to ask … Listen to the conversation. Then, answer the questions.

1. What is Elena's problem? Does she take too much time before asking for her professor's help? Explain your answer. Why does she talk to the professor the way she does?

2. What phrase does Elena use to introduce the complication involving her mother? Why might this second reason be persuasive for the professor?

3. What reason does the professor give for not being able to give the test when Elena asks? Why doesn't Elena start proposing other solutions?

4. What phrases does the professor use to indicate that he wants to find another solution and that he wants Elena's feedback?

5. What phrases does Elena use to show the professor that she appreciates his willingness to compromise?

T. **Happy ending?** With your classmates, think of a topic of conflict that might come up between two people or among a group of people (coworkers, students and teachers, political opponents, a couple, etc.). Discuss the details that people would probably not agree on. Then, role-play a conversation in which you discuss the problem and try to resolve the conflict. Use phrases from the **Communicative Strategies** that you learned in this chapter.

U. **Big decision.** Imagine that you live on a tropical island with exotic plants and animals, beautiful waterfalls, and perfect beaches. You don't have much, but you don't need much. But some people in your community want to invite tourists to the island in order to make money and live more comfortably. Others are against the idea, believing it will ruin the island. Role-play a community meeting in which you discuss the problem and try to reach a compromise. In your discussion, use the **Communicative Strategies** you've learned in this chapter.

 INTERNET RESEARCH Conflicts. Search for online articles and blogs that talk about conflicts in relationships: parents and children, couples, neighbors, coworkers, etc. What advice do people give for solving problems and reaching compromises? Summarize the stories of how people solved the problems they had with others.

8 Hypothesizing and Predicting

"What would happen if …?"

Strategies for Communication

Part 1: How to Hypothesize

Part 2: How to Make Predictions

Part One

PREPARE

A. PRE-LISTENING **Personality test.** For each question below, circle the answer that best describes you. Then, read the information in the box below to find out what your answers reveal about your personality.

1. Imagine you are at a party. What would you be doing there?

   A. I'd be telling jokes and talking to a big group of people.

   B. I'd be in a corner of the room, talking with a friend.

2. What might you do if you had a problem?

   A. I might call a friend for advice.

   B. I might think about it and deal with it the next day.

3. How would you support a cause you're very passionate about?

   A. I would get involved as a volunteer.

   B. I would write letters to the editor of our newspaper or start a blog.

4. You've joined a new group. What would be your role?

   A. I'd probably end up being the leader.

   B. I'd mostly listen to what others have to say.

5. You achieved a goal that you've been working toward for a long time. What would you do next?

   A. I'd let everyone know about my accomplishment.

   B. I'd set another goal for myself right away.

6. Imagine you won a contest. Which prize would you choose?

   A. I'd choose a week in Rio de Janeiro, Brazil, during Carnival.

   B. I'd choose a week hiking in Australia.

7. What career would you prefer if you were really good in chemistry?

   A. I'd be a chemistry teacher so I could share my love of science with as many students as possible.

   B. I'd be a researcher in a lab and try to find a cure for cancer.

Your Personality Results

Count the number of times you answered "A" and the number you answered "B."

More "A's" than "B's":   You're more of an extrovert. You enjoy being with people and don't mind being the center of attention. You like the energy of large crowds. When you're excited about something, you want to share it with others.

More "B's" than "A's":   You're more of an introvert. You care about people, but your favorite way of socializing is having personal conversations with a few friends. You like to analyze your own thoughts and feelings. You enjoy watching how other people interact.

CD 2 Tracks 38–47 **B.** **LISTENING Hypothesis or certainty?** Listen to the sentences. Decide if the speakers are expressing a hypothesis (a possibility) or a certainty (a fact). Check (✓) the appropriate column.

	Hypothesis	Certainty
1.	_____	_____
2.	_____	_____
3.	_____	_____
4.	_____	_____
5.	_____	_____
6.	_____	_____
7.	_____	_____
8.	_____	_____
9.	_____	_____
10.	_____	_____

CD 2 Track 48 **C.** **LISTENING Man's best friend.** Listen to the conversation. Complete the sentences with the missing words as directed.

Add the verbs that are missing from these hypothetical sentences with the word **if**.

1. I wonder if we _____ him another dog.

2. If we _____ him another dog, he _____ we're trying to replace Pepper.

3. But what if he _____ the new dog?

4. I'll bet he _____ better if he _____ more exercise.

5. What _____ if he goes to Florida this winter?

Add the words that are missing from these hypothetical sentences without the word **if**.

6. Do you think he _____ sick or something?

7. But _____ that were true.

8. What _____ do about it?

9. I _____ he would learn to love a new dog.

10. _____ we're getting ahead of ourselves.

COMMUNICATIVE STRATEGIES: *How to Hypothesize*

Dave: If only I had more time!

John: **It looks as though** you have way too much to do.

Dave: There's no doubt about that, but **what can I do** about it?

John: **If I were you**, I'd convince the boss that you need an assistant.

PHRASES

Asking hypothetical questions

What would happen (if) …?

What can / should I do (about it)?

What would you do / suggest?

Do you think I should / could …?

How should / could I … ?

Do you think (it's because) … ?

What would happen if …? / What if …?

Why do you think …?

What could that mean?

Making hypothetical statements

If + *verb*, (then) + would / could / should / might … (If I saw her, I would say hi.)

Must + *verb* (She must have left already.)

If I were you, … / in your shoes, …

Let's say you were to …

I might / could / should / ought to …

(Let's) suppose / say / assume / think about / imagine that …

It looks like / sounds like / seems like / appears that …

I'm guessing / thinking (that) …

Maybe / Possibly it's because …

It's probably because …

I wonder if …

I imagine / suspect …

I'll bet …

Note: See the *Speaker's Handbook* on page 157 for additional phrases.

D. You should … Imagine that someone says the following statements to you. Respond to the comments with two hypothetical statements, using phrases from the **Communicative Strategies**.

Example: "I just saw someone cheating on a test."

You should probably tell your instructor.

You could talk to the student who cheated.

1. "I'd really like to fix up my house."

2. "I'm feeling pretty out of shape these days."

3. "I would love to travel someplace interesting."

4. "Our teacher looks really happy today."

5. "I just found $100 in cash in the parking lot of the grocery store."

6. "Why can't I figure out how this phone works?"

Language Focus: *If*-clauses

In English, hypothetical statements or questions are often expressed with ***if*-clauses**. An *if*-clause can …

- show how something *would be* if certain conditions *were* met.

  If + *simple past* + *modal* + *verb*
  If I *had* a lot of money, I *would build* schools all over the world.
  I *could build* schools all over the world **if** I *had* a lot of money. (The situation is still possible in the future.)

- show how something *might have been* if certain conditions *had been* met.

  If + *past perfect* + *modal* + *present perfect*
  If I *had seen* him there, I *would have told* you.
  I *would have told* you **if** I *had seen* him there. (It's too late to change the situation.)

  Note: The simple past form of the verb **to be** in an *if*-clause is always **were**.

  If he **were** here, he'd tell you the story.   I'd turn back if I **were** you.

E. What if? Write the endings of five hypothetical questions that you could ask someone in order to learn more about him or her. The questions can cover any topics that you think are appropriate. You will ask your classmates these questions in class.

1. What would you do if _____

_____

2. What would you do if _____

_____

3. What would you do if _____

_____

4. What would you have done if _____

_____

5. What would you have done if _____

_____

F. Redo. Think of something in your past that you wish you could do all over again. It can be a decision you made, something you did or didn't do, or a second chance at something. Complete the prompt below and write at least two sentences that explain what you would do differently. Then, write down two hypothetical questions that you would ask a classmate about how they would have handled your situation.

If I could do it all over again, I would _____

_____

_____

What I would do differently: _____

_____

_____

Questions for classmates: _____

_____

_____

👄 TALK 👄

👥 **G. Peer correction.** Compare the responses you wrote for Activity D with those of your classmates. Add any hypothetical responses to your list that you find especially useful.

👥 **H. What if?** Ask a classmate the five hypothetical questions you wrote down in Activity E. Your classmate will respond with hypothetical statements, using phrases from the **Communicative Strategies**. When finished, switch roles.

👥 **I. Redo.** Using the information you wrote in Activity F, tell a classmate about something in your past that you wish you could do all over again. Say what you would do differently. Then, ask your classmate the questions to see how he or she would have handled the situation. When finished, switch roles.

Cultural Connections: Critical Thinking in the Classroom

Students in U.S. schools not only have to learn facts and information in their courses, they are also expected to think critically about their subjects. Critical thinking includes analyzing, hypothesizing, predicting, and asking questions. The purpose of thinking critically is to interpret the meanings behind the facts and try to offer new ideas and perspectives about them. Students who develop their critical  thinking skills often perform better in school and are rewarded with higher grades.

Is critical thinking encouraged in schools where you're from? Are students expected to come up with their own ideas about subjects? What factors contribute to students' grades?

👥 **J. My dream job.** Imagine that you could have any job you wanted. Have a conversation with a classmate in which you both describe your dream jobs. Consider the questions below in your conversation. Use phrases from the **Communicative Strategies** to help you ask and answer hypothetical questions.

Possible questions:

What skills would you need? / How would you prepare for the job? / What would your responsibilities be? / If you have to travel for the job, where would you go? / How much money would you earn? / What would you like to accomplish?

Part Two

●◖ PREPARE ◗●

LISTENING COMPREHENSION: *Hypothesizing vs. Predicting*

As you've learned, a **hypothesis** is something that may or may not be true or become true. A **prediction**, on the other hand, describes something that is likely to happen or not happen. It is important to know if a speaker is hypothesizing or predicting. Here are three things to listen for to help you know the difference.

- **Phrases.** Phrases used to hypothesize are more hesitant or uncertain. Phrases used to predict are more confident and sure.

  Hypothesis: **It looks like** she's coming to class today. (uncertain phrase)

  Prediction: **I'm sure that** she's coming to class today. (certain phrase)

- **Verbs.** Sometimes you can recognize hypotheses and predictions by the verb tenses used.

  Hypothesis: If I **had** the money, I **would pay** the bills.
  (past tense in *if*-clause; conditional mood in main clause)

  Prediction: If I **have** the money, I **will pay** the bills.
  (present tense in *if*-clause; future tense in main clause)

- **Intonation.** The intonation in hypothetical statements can rise or fall. The intonation in statements of prediction always falls.

  ↗   ↘

  Hypothesis: I think he's coming at noon, but I'm not sure.

  ↘

  Prediction: It's likely he's coming at noon.

CD 2
Tracks
49–56

K. LISTENING **Are you sure?** Check (✓) the appropriate box to indicate if the speakers are expressing a hypothesis or a prediction. Then, write down the words that helped you decide each answer.

	HYPOTHESIS	PREDICTION	WORDS THAT SUPPORT YOUR ANSWER
1.			
2.			
3.			
4.			
5.			
6.			
7.			
8.			

CD 2 Track 57 **L.** **LISTENING Cultural exchange.** As you listen to the conversation, write down the verbs you hear. Then, listen again, and for each verb, indicate if the speaker is generalizing (**G**) the way things are, hypothesizing (**H**) the way things could be, or predicting (**P**) the way things will be.

read (G); learn (G);

Language Focus: *If*-Clauses to Express Predictions

In addition to expressing hypotheses, some *if*-clauses can also signal predictions about what will happen. *If* sentences that express predictions are formed like this:

> **If** + *present tense*,   *future tense*
>   (condition)   (prediction)

> **If** you **eat** a lot of sweets, you**'ll get** cavities.

The order of these clauses can be reversed. When the *if*-clause comes after the main clause, do not use a comma.

> We**'ll be able** to buy a house if we **save** our money.

Joey: **What do you think is gonna happen?**

Pablo: Hard to tell. But this is the Rockets, so **there's a good chance** that they'll get beaten in the last inning. That seems to happen to them a lot.

PHRASES

Asking for a prediction

Can you predict …?

What's your prediction?

What do you think will happen?

Do you think …?

Who / What / When / Where / Why will …?

What will happen if …?

What's going to happen (next / now)?

Making a prediction

It's possible / probable / obvious / evident / likely / certain that …

I'll probably / obviously / definitely / never / certainly / always …

I'll bet (you anything) that …

I predict / expect / think / know / believe (that) …

In my opinion / I'm sure that / I doubt that / I'm convinced that …

There's no way … / There's no chance …

For sure … / There's a good chance …

It's a sure thing that …

I'm assuming (that) …

There'll be … / There won't be …

One of these days / Someday / In ten years / By 2050 / Any day / Any minute now / Before we know it / Never in a million years

Note: See the *Speaker's Handbook* on page 157 for additional phrases.

M. And then what? Look at the photos carefully. Predict what will happen as a result of what the people are doing. Use phrases from the **Communicative Strategies** in your answers.

Example: <u>Look at her! She's obviously going to have an accident</u>
<u>any minute now!</u>

1.

_____

_____

_____

2.

3.

_____   _____

_____   _____

_____   _____

_____

4.

5.

_____   _____

_____   _____

_____   _____

_____   _____

N. Conversation starters. For each topic, write two questions that you could ask to have a classmate make predictions. Use phrases from the **Communicative Strategies**.

> **Example:** medical research
>
> *Do you think they'll find a cure for cancer?*
>
> *How long do you think the average person born in 2030 will live?*

1. the classes you'll take next term

2. the career or private life of a famous performer (athlete, movie star, singer)

3. the effects of global warming

4. how changing technology affects people

5. changes in your school or the town you live in

6. your classmate's future plans

O. Headlines. Read the newspaper headlines. Then, write two predictions about what will happen in the future based on the situations mentioned in the headlines.

> **Example:** **No more speed limits on nation's highways**
>
> *It's clear to me that there will be more serious accidents and deaths.*
>
> *People will definitely buy more gas, because it takes more gas to drive fast. ...*

1. **Fewer parents vaccinating children against diseases**

2. No rain in sight, drought enters fourth month

_____

_____

3. All district students promised college scholarships

_____

_____

4. Scientists discover cure for cancer

_____

_____

5. Two factories to close at end of month

_____

_____

Professional Context: Hypothesizing and Predicting in Business

The ability to hypothesize and predict business trends is important to the success of companies. Investors buy shares (or stocks) in businesses when they predict that the value of those companies will go up.

To help people predict whether stock prices might be going up or down, news broadcasts often share statistics about _consumer confidence_. If consumers (people who buy goods) feel optimistic about their own finances, they are more likely to buy things. This raises the demand for the goods and services that companies produce. As a result, their profits and the value of their stocks will go up. If stockholders sell their stock when consumer confidence is high, they will probably receive more money than they paid for it.

On the other hand, things that make stock prices fall include:

- natural disasters
- political unrest
- rumors that a company is in financial trouble
- competition from other companies

●● TALK ●●

P. **Peer correction.** With your classmates, compare the predictions you made in Activity M. Tell your classmates which of their predictions you like best.

Q. **Conversation starters.** Move around the room and ask different classmates the questions you wrote for Activity N. Your classmates will give you predictions based on your questions. Keep the conversation going by reacting and asking for more information.

R. **Worries.** With a classmate, take turns predicting everything you're sure will go wrong in each of the following situations. Use phrases from the **Communicative Strategies**.

Example: You and a friend are going to take a trip to a foreign country.
> **A:** *I'll bet the airline is gonna lose my luggage. They always do …*
> **B:** *Don't you think you're exaggerating? They don't always lose it. What I'm worried about is not being able to understand anyone. My Mandarin isn't all that great.*
> **A:** *So? You're gonna get better really fast once you …*

1. You and a friend are going to take a trip to a foreign country.

2. You tell your friend that you're going to the doctor for a physical exam.

3. You tell your friend that you're going to prepare dinner for your boss.

4. You and your classmate are going to make a class presentation.

S. **Headlines.** Refer to the headlines in Activity O and the predictions you made for each one. Role-play a television interview with a classmate. One of you is a journalist and the other an expert about the subject of each headline. Use phrases from the **Communicative Strategies** for asking for and making predictions.

Example: **No more speed limits on nation's highways**
> **Journalist:** *So tell me, what do you think will happen without speed limits on the highways?*
> **Expert:** *Well, it's clear to me that there will be more serious accidents and more deaths.*
> **Journalist:** *That's not good news. So, you don't approve of this change?*
> **Expert:** *No, I don't. It will be a disaster. People will definitely buy more gas, too, because it takes more gas to drive fast.*
> **Journalist:** *And of course, that will lead to more pollution …*

T. **I know just what will happen.** With a classmate, invent a conversation between the two people in each situation given below. One of you asks many questions about the future, and the other predicts what will happen.

1. two parents talking about their daughter, who just got her driver's license

2. a high school senior asking an older friend what college will be like

3. one family member talking to another who just won a lot of money in the lottery

4. a person speaking with a friend about a trip the friend has suggested

 **IMPROVISE**

U. LISTENING Uh-oh … Listen to the conversation, and then answer the questions.

1. What is this conversation about?

2. What are three predictions the students make about things that they're pretty sure of: how they think things are now or what they think will happen next?

3. What are four hypothetical statements the students make about how things *could be* different or about how things *could have been* different under different circumstances?

4. What are some of the statements Tomas makes about how things generally are (statements that do not apply just to this particular incident)?

5. Would you say that both of the speakers are good students? Why or why not?

V. Will everything work out? Select one of the situations below and role-play it with a classmate.

1. Olivia and Manuel have been going out for a while. You and your friend are wondering how serious their relationship is, whether they're really compatible, how their families might feel about the couple, what their plans for the future might be, etc.

2. You have a new boss. You and a coworker are discussing what it will be like to work for her, what you've already heard about her, what she might do differently compared to your old boss, how long you think she'll stay, what you might do to gain her respect, etc.

3. You and your partner want to start a business. First, decide what kind of business it will be. Then, discuss what products or services it will provide, how you could set up the company, who would handle the various responsibilities of the business, how you would advertise your product, etc.

W. Class discussion: Can this planet be saved? With your class, talk about the environmental problems that concern you the most. Hypothesize and predict what is likely to happen to our planet. Refer to these questions to help your discussion.

- What kind of future do you predict for planet Earth?
- What changes are you making yourself?
- What changes do you still plan to make?
- How could we teach future generations about environmental issues?
- How will the future be different if attitudes don't change?
- How will the future be different if attitudes do change?

Useful Phrases

air pollution / water pollution / noise pollution / smoke stacks / factories' effects on nature / conservation / recycling / reusing / conserving water / endangered wildlife (plants and animals)

 INTERNET RESEARCH What's your ecological footprint? Go online and look for a website, such as www.myfootprint.org, that helps you figure out your "ecological footprint." This is a quiz that tells you if you're using more than your share of the world's resources. After taking the quiz, think about your own lifestyle. Based on the results of the quiz, talk to your classmates about what changes you might make in your life to help the environment.

PRELIMINARY CHAPTER

Activity B: What did you say?, p. 2

Conversation 1

Kyle: Hey, Carlos. How's it going?

Carlos: Fine, how about you? Haven't seen you in a long time. What are you up to?

Kyle: Well, the big news is that I'm studying in South Korea next year.

Carlos: Really? Wow! Congratulations!

Kyle: Yeah, I even got a scholarship that covers housing and food while I'm over there. I'll be living at home with my parents this summer and then I leave in the fall.

Carlos: Did you say you're gonna be there for a whole year?

Kyle: Yeah. And my parents and my little sister are gonna visit me during the December break. Can't wait.

Conversation 2

Susan: Hey, Emma. I want you to meet my friend Alejandro. Alejandro, this is Emma.

Emma: Hello, Alejandro. Nice to meet you.

Alejandro: Nice to meet you, too, Emma.

Susan: Alejandro just got here from Argentina. He's studying mechanical engineering.

Emma: What part of Argentina are you from?

Alejandro: I grew up in Mendoza.

Emma: Oh, I've never been to Mendoza. But I have visited Buenos Aires. I just love Argentina!

Alejandro: How do you and Susan know each other?

Susan: Oh, we've known each other since elementary school. Now we share an apartment with two other friends.

Conversation 3

Inez: OK. So you and I are responsible for bringing the food to the surprise birthday party. What do you think we should do?

Peter: Well, we definitely need a cake. I'm no good at baking. What about you?

Inez: I think we should just buy one. That's much easier.

Peter: Agreed. And then we can buy chips and drinks. I know how to make a Mexican dip that goes really well with chips. And I can make a salad. But we also need something for the barbecue.

Inez: I'll get hotdogs, hamburgers, and veggie burgers for the vegetarians. What kind of salad are you making?

Peter: Just a mixed salad, with greens, carrots, celery, radishes, and maybe some green peppers. I'll make a basic dressing with oil and vinegar.

Inez: That sounds good. You wanna go shopping together?

Peter: Good idea!

Activity C: Getting acquainted, p. 2

Daniel: Nice party, huh? Hi, I'm Daniel.

Ivan: Nice to meet you, Daniel. I'm Ivan. Yes, it is a nice party. It gives me the chance to meet some new people in the company.

Daniel: Are you new here?

Ivan: Yes, I was just hired a month ago.

Daniel: What department are you in?

Ivan: I work in accounting. I got my accounting degree here in Boston and then I was lucky enough to get this job.

Daniel: So you're from Boston?

Ivan: Well, that's where I studied. But I'm from Belarus originally.

Daniel: Um … I'm embarrassed to say that I don't really know where that is. *(chuckles)*

Ivan: That's OK. Most people don't know where Belarus is. It's in Eastern Europe between Russia and Poland.

Daniel: OK, that gives me a good idea. How long ago did you leave Belarus?

Ivan: I've been in the U.S. for 7 years. But I go home to visit my family once or twice a year, and my parents come to visit every once in a while.

Activity I: Subtopics, p. 6

Conversation 1

Joe: Do you like to spend time outdoors?

Lola: Yes, I love it. Um … when I'm at work during the week, I go for a walk in the park during my lunch break, and … um … I spend a lot of time working in my garden. Since I work in an office all week, I really try to spend as much time as possible in the fresh air. I love taking my kids camping during the summer.

Conversation 2

Richard: So do you like what you do for work?

Alvin: Yes, most of the time. Sometimes I have days that are not very interesting, but I really like that I get to interact with customers regularly.

Richard: I'm sure. What else do you like about it?

Alvin: Well, I like that my salary is very good. But the most important thing is that I get along really well with my manager. She's a good mentor, and she gives me a lot of freedom.

Conversation 3

Rayna: You said you spend a lot of time reading. What do you read?

Susan: Um, I guess my favorite books are crime novels. I love trying to figure out who committed the crime.

Rayna: Really? I'm not crazy about that kind of thing. What else do you read?

Susan: I read a lot of historical novels. Novels about real historical events like the American Civil War.

Rayna: That's cool. I love history. Anything else?

Susan: Let's see. Sometimes I read science fiction. I think that's a lot of fun.

Conversation 4

Diane: What are you doing for your vacation this year?

Will: I wish I knew. My kids want to go to our cabin at the lake and my wife thinks we should visit her parents in Maine.

Diane: What about you? What do you wanna do?

Will: To tell you the truth, I'd rather just stay home for once. I'd like to relax and not think about traveling. *(chuckles)* That's my idea of a real vacation.

Activity J: Choices, p. 6

Conversation 1

Jennifer: OK. So we know we're spending this weekend in Boston. Now we should probably decide what we wanna do.

Erica: I'd really like to go to the Museum of Science. The planetarium there is supposed to be awesome. I'm taking an astronomy class next semester … so I think it'd be cool to tour the universe first.

Abby: *(chuckles)* That's fine with me, as long as we also get to the Museum of Fine Arts. There's an exhibit on jewelry there. I looked it up online and it looks amazing. You guys can see other stuff if you like. We could also eat lunch there.

Jennifer: Hm … I guess that sounds OK. I'll go along with those plans as long as we make time to go shopping. I wanna buy some presents. My brother's birthday is coming up and so is my parents' anniversary.

Erica and Abby: Sure!

Erica: That'll be fun.

Abby: No problem. I love shopping.

Conversation 2

Sam: I have no idea what I'm gonna do this summer.

Kristin: What's the problem?

Sam: Well, I have a couple of choices, and they're both good ones. I just don't know how to decide.

Manuel: So let's hear them.

Sam: Well, one thing I could do is work in the genetics lab at the university. They've offered me a job. Since I'm going to college in the fall, this would be great experience. I'd have to be at work all day, Monday through Friday. But I'd be making some money.

Kristin: That sounds pretty good. What's your other option?

Sam: I could help my parents on the farm. They'd be happy to have me home all summer. And, since I'll be far away next year, they obviously want to spend as much time with me as possible. They also wouldn't expect me to work too hard.

Manuel: What do your parents say?

Sam: Whatever I do is OK with them. They want me to decide. Luckily I still have a couple weeks before I have to make up my mind.

Manuel: I'm sure you'll figure it out. I wish I had such great options.

Kristin: Yeah, me too.

Conversation 3

Allison: Hello?

Kelly: Hi Allison. It's Kelly.

Allison: Oh hey, Kelly. What's up?

Kelly: Listen, I have to go to San Francisco for a week or so. My dad's in the hospital and I wanna go visit him and help my mom for a while.

Allison: Oh, I'm sorry about your father. Is he going to be OK?

Kelly: Yeah, he'll be fine. It was just minor surgery and he'll be home by Friday.

Allison: So what can I do?

Kelly: Well … I was wondering if you could take care of my cats while I'm away.

Allison: Sure, no problem. What do I do?

Kelly: Well, you'd have to come over twice a day, in the morning and at dinner and feed them. While you're here, you'd also have to clean their litter boxes. Oh yeah, give them fresh water every night. And I can pay you 30 dollars a day.

Allison: That sounds fair. Why don't I come over tonight and you can show me exactly what to do.

Kelly: Thanks Allie, that'd be great. I'll see you tonight.

Activity Q: Do you have a minute?, p. 11

Aksana: Excuse me Eric, do you have a minute?

Eric: Hi Aksana. Sure, come on in. What can I do for you?

Aksana: Well, since I'm new here, I had some questions about the students in my classes.

Eric: OK. I'll try to answer them.

Aksana: Great, I appreciate it. Um, first, I've noticed a few students who are having some problems understanding what's going on in class. How can I handle that?

Eric: Well, um, we're all required to have office hours. So you should tell the students privately that they can come to your office if they'd like extra help.

Aksana: What if it's a problem with writing?

Eric: Well, uh, you can work with students individually, or you can send them to the Writing Center on campus. The writing tutors there are very good and they can focus on specific writing problems. I send students there often.

Aksana: Good idea. Most of my students need some writing help and I don't have enough time to work with them all individually. So, good. Um, my other question is this: Can I ask students to turn in papers by e-mail? What if they don't have a computer or don't know how to use one?

Eric: Most instructors ask for papers to be sent by e-mail, so I think it's fine to ask your students to do it. And if anyone doesn't have a computer, they can go to the Computer Lab on campus. The lab workers there give workshops on using the computer to write and send papers. I hardly ever have students who need to go through a workshop like that, but it is an option.

Aksana: I'm glad to hear that. I guess that's about it for the moment. If I have some other questions, can I come back to see you about them?

Eric: Absolutely. I needed a lot of help and advice when I was new. I'm happy to be of help.

Aksana: Thanks, Eric.

CHAPTER 1

Activity B: What's your place like?, p. 13

Conversation 1

Lucy: I'm glad you're coming to dinner tomorrow night. I moved into the house two weeks ago and you'll be my first visitor. You know how to get to my place, right?

Amy: Yeah I do. I can't wait to see it! What's it like?

Lucy: Well, it's a fairly small one-story house. It looks a little run down at the moment because it needs a coat of paint. It has the messiest yard on the street and looks as if the grass hasn't been mowed in years. I know it needs a lot of work, but it's in a nice neighborhood that's very quiet. And it's in a very sunny location, so I'll be able to plant a large garden. The house is also the only one with a narrow porch and wooden fence around the yard.

Amy: It sounds perfect for you.

Lucy: You'll like it. It's very cozy and comfortable. But I'm still unpacking, so it's a little cluttered.

Conversation 2

David: I can't believe you moved back to the city. I thought you hated urban living.

Samuel: I know, but I'm glad I did it. I found a place on a very wide street in the historic district. The street is a little noisy, but my apartment is pretty quiet. And the location is fantastic. It's within walking distance to some great restaurants, the public library, a couple of movie theaters, and there's even a gym with an indoor pool. And I have great neighbors. Everyone is very friendly.

David: Wow! Is it really expensive?

Samuel: Well, it *is* a bit expensive. But it just got fixed up, so it was in move-in condition.

David: But how far are you from the office?

Samuel: That's another thing. I sold my car because I don't need it. I can take the bus directly to my office and walk everywhere else. If I want to go away, I can always rent a car.

David: It sounds like you got everything you want. I can't wait to come and visit you.

Activity C: On the first floor … , p. 14

This three-story house is perfect for a large family. In front of the house is a large covered porch that can be used for entertaining.

Behind the house is an in-ground swimming pool with a fence around it.

Through the front door on the first floor is an entryway with a large living room to the right. To the left of the living room and next to the kitchen is the dining room. On the other side of the kitchen, a short hallway leads to a guest bathroom on the left and downstairs to the basement and the laundry room. At the end of the hall a doorway leads to the side of the house and into a patio, a garden, and the garage. From the kitchen, a few steps lead up to the main staircase to the second floor.

Upstairs is another hallway. You'll find three bedrooms and a bathroom off the hallway. The bathroom is on the left, and one small bedroom is directly across from it. The second bedroom is down the hall to the right. The master bedroom is at the end of the hallway, and there is a third bathroom inside through a doorway to the left. In the middle of the hallway next to the bathroom is the staircase to the third floor.

The third floor has one very large room that can be used as a TV room or a playroom for children. Off to the right side of the room is a guest bedroom with a bath.

Besides the many closets, there are storage spaces underneath the staircases and above the third floor in the attic.

Activity J: An American home, p. 20

Marco: Hey Angela. I'm so glad I ran into you. I'd like to ask you a favor.

Angela: Hi, Marco. What can I do for you?

Marco: Well Lydia and I just looked at a house we're interested in buying. Since you're a real estate agent, I wonder if you could come see it with us tomorrow and give us your opinion.

Angela: I think I can do that. Why don't you tell me a little about the house and then I'll also check it out on the Internet.

Marco: Well, first of all, it's in a very safe and nice neighborhood with lots of children. It isn't a huge house, but it seems to have enough space for the four of us. Let's see … um … it's a two-story house with a basement that I could maybe turn into the kids' playroom. That's also where the laundry room is. On the main floor, there's a large kitchen on the left side. From the kitchen, you get downstairs to the basement, but also outside to the deck. Um … to the right of the kitchen is a big living room …

Angela: There's no dining room?

Marco: Actually, no, there isn't. But the kitchen is really big. It's a combination kitchen and dining room.

Angela: OK, what else?

Marco: Off the living room, to the right, is a half bath. The stairs to the second floor are in the back of the living room. On the second floor, on the left, there are two very small bedrooms and a bathroom. On the right is the master bedroom with a bathroom.

Angela: What about storage space?

Marco: It's not great. But there's a closet in each bedroom and there's plenty of room in the basement.

Angela: It sounds a little small for the two of you with two young children. But if the price is right, this might be the perfect starter home for you. Why don't I meet you over there tomorrow about 10 and we'll see.

Marco: Thanks, Angela. I appreciate it.

Activity K: How do I get there?, pp. 20–21

Mike: Hey Stephanie, I've got a little problem. I'm calling from Marietta, but guess what? I left my GPS at home and I don't know how to get to the aquarium. Do you think you can help me?

Stephanie: Yeah, no problem. We're already here waiting for you. You're only about half an hour away, depending on the traffic.

Mike: I'll never get there unless you give me good directions. I'm parked, so I can write it all down.

Stephanie: OK, ready? First, you head south on West Park Square toward Whitlock Avenue Northwest. Then you almost immediately take the first left onto South Park Square Southeast.

Mike: Was that the first left?

Stephanie: Yeah, that's right. *(slight pause)* OK, then you continue onto Roswell Street and, after about a mile, you turn right onto Cobb Parkway Southeast. You'll have to pay attention here because you'll take a slight left onto South Marietta Parkway Southeast. Got it so far?

Mike: Yeah, I'm good. Then what?

Stephanie: You take the ramp onto I-75 South. You'll go for almost 15 miles and then take exit 249C toward the aquarium.

Let's see … uh, you then turn right onto Ivan Allen Junior Boulevard. Then you'll know you're close. Turn left onto Centennial Olympic Park Drive Northwest and then take the first right onto Baker Street Northwest. The aquarium is on the right. There are signs for the parking lot.

Mike: OK, got it. That doesn't sound too bad. Where do we meet you?

Stephanie: We'll be at the restaurant having lunch. See you soon.

Activity R: A visit to Paris, p. 25

Robert: Hey, Olivia. I had heard that you were back from Paris. Did you have a good time?

Olivia: I had a great time. Paris is an amazing city. It's beautiful, has a lot of history but also with a very modern atmosphere. And the night life is awesome. It *is* like most cities: noisy and very crowded and everything. But, you know, that also made it really exciting.

Robert: Here, let's sit down; you can tell me all about it. *(to a server)* Hi, can we get two cups of coffee please?

Olivia: So where do I start?

Robert: OK, where did you stay?

Olivia: Well, most of the hotels in Paris are pretty expensive, so I stayed in a small hotel in the student quarter. It was in a very old building, had four floors with a really small elevator and very narrow stairs. And the room wasn't very big but it was sunny and cheerful. The bathroom had a tiny shower. But the good thing about this hotel was that it was very clean, the owner was friendly and helpful, and she served a great breakfast every morning.

Robert: How long did you stay in Paris?

Olivia: Two weeks. I totally played the part of tourist! I went to the top of the Eiffel Tower—I found out it was built for the 1889 World's Fair, which I didn't know. Anyway, I walked everywhere. I sat in cafés and parks. I went to some wonderful restaurants. I spent time in the museums, and I practiced my French everywhere I went.

Robert: That's cool. What did you do in the evenings?

Olivia: I went out with my Parisian friends almost every night. There's a lot to do in the city, and it's easy to get around on the subway. Some evenings we just walked along the river. The weather was perfect the whole time. I just loved it!

Robert: It sounds like Paris has become your favorite city.

Olivia: Well, maybe. It has a lot in common with San Francisco, except it's flat while San Francisco is very hilly. And, of course, San Francisco is on the water. But from a cultural point of view the two cities are a lot alike. And the night life is great in both places.

CHAPTER 2

Activity B: Rumor has it, p. 28

Manny: Lupe, can you believe this? This website says there's a sale on plane tickets to Jamaica. Only $180 round-trip!

Lupe: Wow, that's amazing! Be sure to tell Shreena if you see her. She and her friend Dave were looking for a cheap place to go for spring break.

…

Manny: Have you heard that prices for airline tickets to Jamaica are really cheap right now? Tell Shreena and Dave if you see them. They want to go there for spring break.

Ali: Sure thing. I'll pass on the message.

…

Ali: Hey guys, we need to talk about what we're doing for spring break. I think Shreena and Dave are going to Jamaica. I've heard that's a really popular vacation spot for people who just got married.

Keith: Jamaica! Wow, they're lucky. I'm sure they'll have a really good time.

…

Keith: Hey, what do you think of this? Dave and Shreena are getting married, and they're going to spend their honeymoon in Jamaica!

Chelsey: No way! I had no idea they were even a couple! I thought they had just been really good friends since they were kids. In fact, the other night I saw Shreena kissing Dylan. How come I *never* know what's going on!

…

Chelsey: Hey, Shreena, congratulations! I just heard that you and Dave are getting married, and that you're spending your honeymoon in Jamaica. That's great! But … when did you break up with Dylan?

Shreena: WHAT?!?

Activity C: What do you think?, p. 28

(phone ringing)

Ms. Jones: Hello?

Anna: Hello, Ms. Jones, this is Anna Terry. I'm sorry to call you at home. Is this a bad time?

Ms. Jones: Hi, Anna. We're watching the game, but it's halftime, so I have a few minutes. What's up?

Anna: Well, you'll never guess what I just read on the Internet! There's a local group that gives small grants to help after-school programs buy materials they need. What do you think about applying for some of that money?

Ms. Jones: I think that's great! We were just saying that we need more books for beginning readers. I think you should apply.

Anna: OK! I'll look into it tomorrow!

Ms. Jones: And, um … turning to another topic for a minute, didn't you say you would be bringing some of your friends to help with after-school tutoring?

Anna: Yes, I did say that, but I'm having a hard time finding people. I can't understand why more people don't volunteer, can you?

Ms. Jones: Well, I suppose there are several reasons … Oh, excuse me, hold on a second. OK,

be right there! Sorry, my husband says the game's back on. Could you come over to my office tomorrow afternoon at around 3:00? We'll discuss how you write up a grant proposal.

Anna: Perfect. I appreciate your willingness to help me. Goodbye, and have a nice evening!

Ms. Jones: Thanks for calling. I'll see you tomorrow.

Activity I: Are we going or not?, p. 32

Joe: Hey, sleepyhead, wake up! I brought you some coffee.

Mary: Hmm? Oh, thanks. That's really sweet of you. *(yawns)* It's so hard to get up Saturday mornings, but I guess it's time.

Joe: Yeah it is. Um, we need to decide whether we're going to the picnic today so I can let David know. He's bringing the burgers to grill, and he needs to know how many people are coming.

Mary: Oh, right! I completely forgot to call him, didn't I? Well, I'd like to go, unless it rains. Have you heard the forecast for this afternoon?

Joe: Do *you* ever believe what they say on TV? Even though the weather report is good, I see some dark clouds out there.

Mary: Yeah, now see, that's a problem for me. I love picnics, but I do *not* want to be outside in bad weather. I'm kind of a wimp, I guess.

Joe: If you're a wimp, I am too. I mean, who wants to get all wet? OK, well, I'm bringing this up now, because we're supposed to bring a dessert. If we're not going, I'd better call David right away.

Activity J: A case of nerves, p. 32

Rita: You know, I've been looking forward to this date forever, and now I'm not even sure I want to go! I feel so stressed out. What's wrong with me?

Charlie: That's my little sister—always worrying! Here, let me be your psychologist for a minute.

"Ms. Shaw, please tell me your feelings so that I can tell you what's wrong with you."

Rita: Charlie! Knock it off unless … you want a punch in the arm.

Charlie: OK, OK. Look, I know you don't know this guy really well, but Andre's a good friend of mine. He's nice, easy to talk to, and he's really into literature. And since you're an English major, you'll have a lot to talk about!

Rita: I guess so. It's just that I keep thinking about Shaun. I miss him.

Charlie: Shaun? Really? You have to stop thinking about him because he broke up with you three months ago. It's time for you to move on.

Rita: I know, you're right. Well, I'll give Andre a try as long as you tell me everything he says about me later!

Charlie: Ha! No promises there!

Activity S: Cultural differences, p. 37

Cathy: That was pretty interesting what Professor Roberts said about how each neighborhood has its own identity.

Arin: Hey, speaking of neighbors, I want to ask you something. Do you guys get along with your neighbors?

Brian: Yeah, mine are pretty cool. We hang out sometimes.

Cathy: I don't know mine that well, but they're always very friendly to me. Why, what about yours?

Arin: Well, actually I think my neighbors are kinda rude, and it's really making me crazy.

Cathy: Really? Well what exactly do you mean by "rude?"

Arin: So, they've lived next door for over a year, right. I hardly ever see them, except when they're walking from the house to their car. They never look at me, they never say "hi." They … they don't even smile at me, really.

Brian: That *is* rude, isn't it?

Cathy: Um, what about their cultural background? Are they from a different country?

Brian: What does that have to with anything? That doesn't matter.

Cathy: Sure it does! Sometimes when you're dealing with people from other cultures, what seems like rudeness to you might have another explanation.

Brian: Like what? Can you give us an example?

Cathy: OK. I have a friend whose dad is from Peru. Sometimes when I see him, he'll say to me, "Cathy, you've really gained weight!"

Brian: Wow, that would make me mad.

Cathy: But he's really not being rude. In Peru, saying someone is overweight is a way of saying they look happy, well fed. In fact, this one time, I—

Arin: Hold on, we're getting off track here. To answer your question about my neighbors, yes, they're from another country, but I'm not sure which one.

Cathy: See, that might be it. I've read that in certain cultures, it's a sign of respect not to make eye contact, especially when you're talking to an older person. But the way I was raised, if you don't look somebody in the eye, they think you're lying to them or hiding something.

Brian: That must be why Arin wouldn't look at me when I asked to borrow her car and she told me it was being repaired. It's cultural!

Arin: What?! I wasn't lying! It had a flat tire!

Brian: Just kidding.

Arin: Anyway, that's a good point, Cathy. Maybe there are cultural differences with my neighbors. Still, I wish they would at least say, "hello." I think I should keep trying to be friendly with them. What do you think?

Cathy: I agree. Just smile and give a little wave whenever you see them. If they start smiling or waving back, then one day maybe you could try to start a conversation with them about their flowers or the weather or something like that. The important thing is that you're trying.

Brian: And if that doesn't work, I'll come over and tell them a few jokes.

Arin: Oh, you'd actually have to be funny first.

CHAPTER 3

Activity B: What and how?, p. 39

Instructions 1

OK. First, you put the clothes in and make sure that the door is closed. Then you move this knob, see, this one here, to select the temperature. Then you turn this knob to pick the setting you want: delicate … regular … quick … whatever. Then you push the start button. It should take only about a half hour. When it's done, all you have to do is fold and put away the clothes.

Instructions 2

Before you start, make sure that you've turned off the power. You don't want to get an electric shock. OK, now you remove the two screws from the small plate, this one at the top and that one at the bottom. Next, you just lift out the old unit, disconnect the two wires, and get rid of it. Where's the new one? … OK, the next thing you do is connect the wires, push the unit back in, attach the plate with the screws and, voilà, you're all set. Let's test it. Go turn on the power. … Did you hear that? Good as new. Next time someone shows up at your door, you'll hear them and they won't wonder why you're not answering when they push the button.

Instructions 3

It's really easy to do this, especially if you have a picture as a model. Let's think about what it looks like from the side. The first step is to draw the front of the face, including the ear. Second, you draw the back of the head and the line down towards the body. Then you sketch the back down to the place where the tail is. OK. The next thing to do is to draw the front, like this. Since this is a side view, you're putting in just one front and one rear leg. Finally, fill in all the lines and add an eye and the tail. See, doesn't that look like Fluffy? The only thing this one can't do is meow.

Instructions 4

Hm … this looks very formal. Let's see what it's all about. It's a nice card and you're supposed to RSVP. What does that mean? Well, it's actually French and it means "Answer please." See, here they show you what to do. You can RSVP by doing it online … this is the website … or you can call … here's the number … or you can even send this card back. If you do that, don't forget to check off "yes" or "no" here. If you say "yes," also write down if you're going alone or bringing a guest to the wedding.

Instructions 5

Let me show you how to make this. It's really easy and you'll love it. We need a mango, a tomato, and a red onion. You can dice the mango and the tomato, and I'll slice the onion. I'll let you make the dressing. Whisk together 2 tablespoons of cilantro, 1 tablespoon of vinegar, 1 tablespoon of fresh lemon juice, and a little salt and pepper. OK, that's great. Now, pour the dressing over the mango mixture. Mix everything together, but do it very carefully. Now, it goes into the refrigerator until you're ready to eat dinner. Just before you serve it, cut the avocado into chunks and stir it in. Serve it over shredded lettuce. This will go perfectly with the fish you're serving.

Instructions 6

Here's what I want you to do. The best way to begin is to go to the library and research the topic both on the Internet and in books and articles. As you read the information, make notes and learn as much as you can about the topic. Be careful: if you write down sentences directly, you have to give the source. When you're done researching, think about the topic and decide what aspect of it you want to write about. The next thing you do is make an outline. That helps you organize your thoughts. Once you're done with that, you can write the first draft. After that, edit and rewrite it until you're satisfied. Remember, this is due by October second and you have to send it to me electronically.

Activity C: How to … , p. 39

Jaime: Can you show me how to transfer the pictures from my camera to my computer?

Kristin: Sure, no problem. Why don't you turn on the computer and I'll show you.

Jaime: OK, it's all set.

Kristin: Before you start, you need the USB cord that connects the camera to the computer. Do you have it?

Jaime: Yeah. This is what came with the camera.

Kristin: Perfect. So, the first thing you do is … let's see … yeah, attach the smaller plug on the USB to your camera, like this. Then you plug in the wider part into one of the outlets on the computer.

Jaime: Nothing's happening.

Kristin: That's because now you have to turn on the camera. If you don't do that, it won't work, so don't forget that step. OK. Um … now the camera's on. See the icon on the bottom of the screen? That's the camera. Just click on it.

Jaime: Wait. Do I click on it once or twice?

Kristin: Just once. Are you writing all this down so you remember for next time?

Jaime: Yeah. I'm trying, but you're going kinda fast.

Kristin: Sorry. We're almost there. OK, see this? We're in the camera. The next thing you do is click twice on that file folder and there are your pics. Now, before you can copy them, you have to open the pictures folder. Go down here, click, and, voilà, we're ready to copy. So here's how you highlight the pics on the camera. And finally, once you've highlighted them, you just drag

them over to the picture folder. See? Like this. And we're done. Oh … and don't forget to turn off the camera before you unplug it from the computer.

Jaime: Got it, thanks! But … I think I'm going to have to go over this again with you.

Kristin: Why don't you take some more pictures and try it on your own. If you're having problems, we can do it together. But I'm sure you'll figure it out.

Activity J: What are the steps?, p. 45

Instructions 1

Before you start the dishwasher, you have to make sure that you've put soap into the compartment inside the door. After that, you close the door and select the water temperature.

Instructions 2

This table is really easy to put together. Make sure you have all the pieces. But before that, let's read the instructions so we can get the right tools. OK. Now you can build the table. First, turn the table top upside down on the floor. After that, screw the legs into the table top.

Instructions 3

No, that's the second thing you should do. First you have to connect the camera to the computer. And *then* you can turn on the camera so that the icon shows up on the computer screen.

Instructions 4

To make a good omelet, you have to follow a few steps very carefully. It helps if you take the eggs out of the refrigerator so that they can get to room temperature before you use them. In the meantime, you can cut up some onions and any other vegetables you want to put into the omelet. Melt some butter in a frying pan and lightly cook the vegetables. While that's happening, you can break the eggs into a bowl and stir them with a fork. Add some salt and pepper to the eggs before scrambling them with the vegetables.

Activity K: Important Details, p. 46

Instructions 1

Before you start the dishwasher, you have to make sure that you've put soap into the compartment inside the door. After that, you close the door and select the water temperature.

Instructions 2

This table is really easy to put together. Make sure you have all the pieces. But before that, let's read the instructions so we can get the right tools. OK. Now you can build the table. First, turn the table top upside down on the floor. After that, screw the legs into the table top.

Instructions 3

No, that's the second thing you should do. First you have to connect the camera to the computer. And *then* you can turn on the camera so that the icon shows up on the computer screen.

Instructions 4

To make a good omelet, you have to follow a few steps very carefully. It helps if you take the eggs out of the refrigerator so that they can get to room temperature before you use them. In the meantime, you can cut up some onions and any other vegetables you want to put into the omelet. Melt some butter in a frying pan and lightly cook the vegetables. While that's happening, you can break the eggs into a bowl and stir them with a fork. Add some salt and pepper to the eggs before scrambling them with the vegetables.

Activity Q: What are they talking about?, p. 52

Instructions 1

I'm going to show you the best way to take care of your teeth. Before you start, take at least 5 minutes to brush your teeth thoroughly. Use an electric toothbrush if you have one. When you're done brushing, cut off a fairly long piece of floss. Wrap the floss around one finger of each hand and push it up between the teeth.

Work it up and down between the two teeth. Once you're done, rinse your mouth with mouthwash. You need to do this at least twice a day, or after each meal if you can.

Instructions 2

OK. So here's how you make these things. We already bought all the ingredients, so it won't take too much time. I would start by chopping some onions and cooking them lightly in a frying pan. Then you add the hamburger. Cook it all the way through. While it's cooking, you can add this package of seasoning and a half a cup of water. Let all this cook. If it looks too dry, just add a little more water. Now you chop all the vegetables: the lettuce, more onions, tomatoes, and anything else you think people might like. I think we'll let everyone serve themselves. Put the pan with the seasoned meat over here. Arrange the bowls with each vegetable around the pan. And don't forget to put out the hot sauce. Oh, I almost forgot. Here are some hard corn shells. We also have some flour tortillas in case people prefer those.

CHAPTER 4

Activity B: What section of the newspaper?, p. 55

Conversation 1

A: Do you know when they're going to start giving flu shots?
B: Yeah, I just saw it in the paper. You can get them in pharmacies starting on the 15th.

Conversation 2

A: Was there anything interesting in the paper this morning?
B: There were several stories about the riots in Europe again. A lot of people have been arrested in several countries.

Conversation 3

A: Listen to this. It says here that many Americans don't get enough vitamin D.

B: Yeah, I read that too. Vitamin D is very important for bones. But I don't think you have to worry about that. You spend a lot of time in the sun in your job. So I'm sure you get plenty of vitamin D.

Conversation 4

A: What's the latest on the local candidate?

B: Well, according to what it says here, he doesn't have much of a chance. He never really answers the interviewers' questions, so it's hard to know what he stands for.

Conversation 5

A: Have you heard about what's happening in the European financial markets?

B: Yeah, from what I've read, it doesn't look good for European banks and the euro.

Conversation 6

A: Who won the game last night?

B: Let's see. Let me find the scores. Here they are. We won eight to six.

Conversation 7

A: It says here that Milwaukee is one of the nicest cities in the U.S. to visit.

B: Really? That's interesting. I've never been to Milwaukee, but …

A: The city is right on Lake Michigan; it's beautiful.

Conversation 8

A: This is absolutely crazy!

B: What is?

A: It says here that hackers have managed to get into practically every computer system in the world. That's really scary.

Activity C: A piece of news, p. 56

Conversation 1

A: Is there anything new in the paper about the break-ins around here?

B: Let me look. Nothing on the front page. OK, here we go. It says here that the police have some very good leads and that they're going to make arrests sometime soon.

A: That's not telling us much. Does it say what kinds of leads?

B: Of course not. They wouldn't tell us that.

A: Well, do they explain how they got the leads?

B: Actually, yes. According to this article, they got quite a few anonymous phone tips.

Conversation 2

A: Good grief! Listen to this! They've recalled the brand of tomato sauce that we buy.

B: Do they give any details? Like expiration dates, numbers to look for …

A: According to this, all of the cans that have a batch number higher than 3660 have been recalled.

B: Well, let's look at the cans we have. Uh, what are we supposed to do if we find any that are bad?

A: Hm, it says here that we should take them to any grocery store and we'll get a refund.

B: By the way, what's wrong with the sauce?

A: All it says is that they found some kind of contamination that can make you really sick.

Conversation 3

A: Wow, I wish we had invested in the social media companies.

B: Really? Why do you say that?

A: Well, because this website says the social media have taken over the way that people communicate.

B: What does that mean, "taken over?"

A: According to this article, it means that people are talking less and less on the phone and instead are posting their personal news to friends and family on social networks.

B: Interesting. Is everybody doing this?

A: It says here that almost everyone's doing it by now. But it's especially popular with young people.

B: That makes sense. But if I want to ask my parents for money, I'm still gonna call them. I don't want all *my* friends to know I'm poor.

Activity J: One question at a time, p. 60

1

… a report filed by police. Because of the recent home break-ins, residents are asked to make sure that they keep their doors and windows locked when they're not home. This alert applies to everyone living in the western suburbs, including the town of Spatterdock. In other news, the director of …

2

… incident yesterday morning. Harold's Gym has been closed until further notice after an elderly driver accidentally drove her car through the gym's front windows. The driver's car landed in the gym's indoor pool. No one was injured in the accident, but it will take at least two weeks for the window to be repaired and for the gasoline and oil to be cleaned from the pool. In sports, the Detroit Red Wings …

3

… something to see this week. Acclaimed director Miles Shaw and his talented crew will arrive in town today to begin shooting their latest documentary. Shaw is known for such award-winning documentaries as *Flight of the Falcon* and *Over Here*. Local residents who would like …

4

… and discovered items missing. The robbers managed to get away with the couple's coin collection and some valuable jewelry. According to police, they got into the apartment by dressing up as workers from the electric company and claiming to be fixing a power failure in the building. It is believed that the suspects …

5

… four incidents in the past month. There are a few things you can do to make sure you're safe when jogging in the park. First, go jogging there only during the day, because there are very few people in the park after dark. Also, always let someone know that you're going out and where you're going. And, finally, carry a phone and a whistle. If you think you're in danger, call 911 immediately. On a lighter note, the Strawberry Festival …

6

… crews worked all night. The power failures during the storm affected many towns in the region for several hours. According to the electric company, power was out in most areas between 2 and 6 a.m. Except for a few neighborhoods, power was restored everywhere by 9 a.m. Another storm system is expected …

Activity K: I just heard . . . , p. 60

Good morning. You're listening to *The Joanne Freeman Show*. In an incident last week that has gained national attention, four teenagers from Omaha used a car and skateboards to imitate a stunt they had seen on television. The four boys, whose names have been withheld because of their ages, took turns riding behind the car on their skateboards with a rope tied around their waists and to the car's bumper. They reportedly got the idea from a recent episode of "Daredevils," the reality TV show that features real people doing dangerous stunts for money.

For the four Omaha teens, reality almost became tragedy. While reaching speeds up to 25 miles an hour through the city streets, one of the boys fell off his skateboard and was dragged along the pavement for 50 yards before the driver stopped the car. One of his friends immediately called 911 with his cell phone, and the injured boy was taken by ambulance to Nebraska Medical Center. He was treated for severe cuts on his arms and legs and a concussion, but he is expected to make a full recovery. When questioned by police, the other teens said they were trying to be "Daredevils" so they could be on TV.

And so the question remains: has reality television gone too far? We know that television viewing is one of the most popular ways that people in the United States spend their free time. According to one statistic, Americans spend one-third of their free time watching TV, and 67 percent of that time is spent watching reality shows. It's also estimated that 99 percent of American households have at least one television, and a majority of homes have three or more.

The incident in Omaha has opened a bigger debate about the influence of television viewing on young people. Could this skateboarding accident have been avoided if the teens hadn't seen the stunt first on "Daredevils"? Is reality television creating a generation of young people who believe fame is more important than safety? Who is responsible for putting limits on what kids watch on TV? The phone lines are open, 555-7777. Let us know what you think.

Activity S: Missing for a month, p. 67

And here's the remarkable story of Bruno, a dog who had an amazing adventure in the cold New Hampshire woods.

One month ago, Claire Newcomb was driving along highway 91 with her beloved dog Bruno on her way to visit family in New Hampshire for Thanksgiving. It was a difficult travel day. A storm had moved into the area, with severe downpours and wind gusts up to 50 miles an hour. The heavy traffic made the situation even more hazardous, and many drivers pulled to the side of the road to wait out the storm.

Claire moved along very slowly when, without warning, a semi from behind ran into her and sent her car over an embankment. The car rolled over several times. When the police arrived, Claire was unconscious and Bruno, a Maltese, was gone. The dog had evidently jumped out of the open window and disappeared into the woods.

Claire was taken to the local hospital where she was treated for numerous injuries, but none of them life-threatening. When she regained consciousness, her first question was, "Where's Bruno?" Her family had to tell her the bad news that her canine companion had run away from the accident scene. Claire begged everyone to keep searching. Posters were put up throughout the region, veterinary clinics and animal shelters were notified, and the family ran ads on the local radio station and in the newspaper. But Bruno was nowhere to be found.

After several days, Claire left the hospital, but she could not accept the idea that Bruno was gone. She stayed in a local hotel, continuing the search for Bruno on her own. As she recovered from her injuries, she took long walks around the area, repeatedly calling Bruno's name. Finally, after more than a week, she had to return home.

Claire was beginning to give up hope until one morning she received a call from a family in Northern New Hampshire. Against all odds, Bruno had appeared on their front porch, dirty, very skinny, covered in twigs and leaves, but with no visible injuries. The family called Claire's phone number, which was printed on Bruno's collar, to let her know that Bruno had been found and was now under the care of a local vet. Claire's life suddenly changed for the better. She drove back up to New Hampshire and was reunited with her best friend, who is once more safe and sound in his own home.

But questions remain about how Bruno survived for a month in the woods of New Hampshire. How did he avoid the coyotes that roam this region? What did he find to eat? Where did he find shelter? Regardless of the unanswered questions, this is one story of survival with a very happy ending.

CHAPTER 5

Activity B: Will they or won't they?, p. 70

Conversation 1

Beth: Hey, I thought we were supposed to go out tonight.

Steve: Oh, yeah, I guess we were. Uh, I'm exhausted. It's been a long week.

Beth: I know, but we did tell Sun-Young we'd meet her at Sagarino's at 10:00 …

Steve: You're right, you're right. I'll get my jacket.

Conversation 2

Will: Uh, do you really think you should be doing that?

Jim: What? Why not? And why do you care?

Will: Well don't you think the zoo animals are on a special diet or something?

Jim: Oh don't be so uptight. I'm not hurting them. It's only bread.

Conversation 3

Delia: Listen, I really need to return this briefcase.

Clerk: I'm sorry, miss. No returns after 60 days. That's the policy.

Delia: I know, but this was a gift for my birthday three months ago, and I had put it away until just yesterday and I noticed this big scratch in the leather.

Clerk: Hm, let's see. *(pause)* Ah, yes, there it is. OK, let me ask my manager if we can make an exception for you.

Conversation 4

Mrs. Ayers: Hi Janice. Would you consider babysitting for us this evening? Our sitter just called and canceled on us.

Janice: Oh, gosh, I'm not sure. I have a lot of work to do tonight. Um, I suppose I could bring my computer over …

Mrs. Ayers: It would be a big help to us. Tell you what—we'll make sure the kids are in bed by the time you get here. With any luck, you'll have peace and quiet all evening.

Conversation 5

Adam: Jeannie, you guys should hire John for your sales position.

Jeannie: Why? Do you think he'd be good?

Adam: That goes without saying. He's got tons of experience, and everybody in the area knows him.

Jeannie: Well, we're looking for someone with more international experience. I appreciate the suggestion though!

Activity C: An offer you can't refuse, p. 70

Matt: Hey, did you see that the company will give us time off if we want to finish college? I'm gonna do it. You should too.

Skip: No way. I just couldn't manage it.

Matt: What do you mean? Why not?

Skip: Well, I couldn't afford it. Even with both of us working, there's not much left over at the end of the month.

Matt: No, no, you need to realize that this is time off with pay.

Skip: With pay? Really? How do you know that?

Matt: It says it right there in the announcement they sent out. You just didn't read it carefully enough.

Skip: Guess I just skimmed through it 'cause I thought I wasn't gonna have the time to take advantage of it. I barely see my kids as it is.

Matt: Mm, that is tough, I agree. But the fact is, if you get your degree, you'll get paid a little more and there's a chance for better jobs within the company.

Skip: Well, that's true.

Matt: Look, you said you wanted to start going to night school at some point so you could finish up.

Skip: I know, but I think I'm just too tired to do it. By the time I'm done at work every day, I'm just too tired to …

Matt: But don't you see? This would be during the day, not at night. Of course, you'll have to study at night, but you could still see your kids.

Skip: Hm, you've got a point there.

Matt: And you'll feel good knowing you worked hard to get your degree. Don't you think it's worth pushing yourself a little bit?

Skip: Yeah, I guess you're right. Still, it's been a long time since I've been in a classroom. I wonder if I still know how to study, write papers …

Matt: Of course you do. You're one of the smartest people I know. Besides, if we take the same classes, we can study together.

Skip: OK, OK, you can stop now. You've convinced me. I just need to get used to the idea. And figure out how to get there.

Matt: That should be no problem either. I'll drive.

Skip: OK, then, let's do it. And as one future manager to another, let me compliment you on how you just managed me!

Activity K: Which is it?, p. 76

1

The game starts at 8:00. Carlos might go with us, …?

2

I can't believe the president was in town. Did you see him, …?

3

It's time to register for classes. I could take biology this semester, …

4

This is a pretty easy task. If I can do it, …

5

Don't worry about it too much. If he doesn't call you, …

Activity L: A bit confusing, p. 76

Stan: Ray, you gotta hear this story. So Ariel called me last night. She said Eric asked her out at Brian's party Friday night.

Ray: He did? But I thought he was dating Julie.

Stan: No, Julie is with Ben, not Eric. Eric was dating Sarah, but they broke up.

Ray: So Eric is single. And he asked out Ariel. But isn't Ariel with Mark?

Stan: No, Ariel and Mark are friends. They never dated.

Ray: So Ariel is single too?

Stan: No, Ariel is going out with Brian. Eric asked Ariel out at his party!

Ray: Whoa, that's bold! Why would he do that?

Stan: I don't know. But I heard that Brian kissed Sarah.

Ray: Interesting. Was this at the party?

Stan: No, at school.

Ray: So Eric heard about it, went to the party, and asked Ariel out. What did she say?

Stan: What do you think she said?

Ray: I hope she said no.

Stan: Wrong. She said yes, and here's the kicker. She doesn't know about the kiss.

Ray: And how do you know that?

Stan: Because she didn't mention it to me when she called.

Ray: So maybe it's not true. In fact … ugh, you know what, this is too confusing. I'm hungry. Let's get a burrito.

Activity S: Are you sure about that?, p. 81

Jonathan: See you later, Mom. I'm going downtown with Cristina and Mike.

Mother: Have fun! Hey, are you going shopping, or are you just having dinner?

Jonathan: Well … Mike needs some stuff. And, uh … there's this jacket …

Mother: A jacket? But you already have your black one! It's perfectly fine. I'm not sure it's a good idea to spend your money on something like that right now.

Jonathan: I know, I know. But it's on sale, and it's a really good deal. It's 60 percent off. Three hundred dollars is an amazing deal for a leather jacket!

Mother: Leather? I thought you said you weren't going to wear leather anymore.

Jonathan: Well, yeah, but …

Mother: And isn't $300 more than you'd normally pay for a jacket?

Jonathan: It is, but you have to understand …

Mother: And what about the fact that it's going to cost you a fair amount of money every time you have it cleaned?

Jonathan: I guess you're right. I hadn't really thought about that … And it already has a little stain on it. Maybe that's why it's on sale. But I still really want it.

Mother: Well, I guess it's up to you. Still, I think it's impractical. Besides, won't it take most of the money you earned from your part-time job?

Jonathan: Probably. But you have to admit that leather lasts a really long time.

Mother: If you take care of it.

Jonathan: Come on, Mom. Why are you telling me how to spend my money? And you know I always take good care of my things …

Mother: Look, Jonathan, let's not argue about it. I can see you're not convinced. But could I just ask you to think it over?

Jonathan: All right, I'll tell you what. I won't buy it *today*. Fair enough?

Mother: Fair enough. At least we know where we stand.

Jonathan: I see myself standing with a new leather jacket! OK, OK, don't look at me like that! I was kidding.

CHAPTER 6

Activity B: What type of art is it?, p. 84

1
Look at the colors and the details in the one on the left. The blue is particularly striking. Especially when the sun shines through it in the late afternoon.

2
On this canvas, the artist really captures daily life in a small town. She uses colors and shapes to suggest the streets, the buildings, and the people going about their everyday business.

3
These pieces were found in a tomb. They're made of solid gold, and the complicated designs on them show that they belonged to a very wealthy woman.

4
Is it art or vandalism? You can decide. This artist has painted images on skateboard ramps all over the country and the skateboarders have a lot of respect for him. But nobody knows his identity.

5
It's clear that he prefers black and white over color images. Here you see the landscapes where he creates special effects by using a variety of lenses.

6
We really don't know who created these works of art. But it's clear that they wanted to show what was important in their lives. Like the hunters and the animals.

Activity C: Van Gogh's bedroom, p. 85

Margaret: This is one of my very favorite paintings by Van Gogh. I even bought a print of it and framed it for my office.

Jack: What do you like about it?

Margaret: Well, look at it. It's a bedroom in Van Gogh's house. Simple, right? But when you really study it, you realize that it has other layers and meanings.

Jack: I don't know much about art, so I can't really describe a painting.

Margaret: That's OK. But you can say whether you like it or not and why, right?

Jack: Sure. Um … I think I like it. It's … uh … it looks like a very comfortable and warm room. Hm. It has a very calming effect. It feels peaceful and quiet.

Margaret: Exactly. What else?

Jack: Well, I like the colors. The walls and doors are different shades of blue and give an impression of coolness. But everything else feels much warmer. Like the reds, yellows, browns, and just a splash of green. Let's see … The furniture looks solid. I, uh, can imagine sleeping in the bed. It looks soft and comfortable.

Margaret: I think that's exactly what van Gogh wanted to show. This was a guest room in his house and he wanted his friends to be comfortable.

Jack: But there's also something strange about the whole thing. How are you supposed to get in and out? The doors are blocked by a chair and the bed. Seems odd.

Margaret: Hmm, maybe that's the way he wanted to show that the guest would have privacy.

Jack: And all the furniture is crammed into the far side of the bedroom. The rest of the room is practically empty.

Margaret: That part's called the foreground. Yeah, good observation. I'm not really sure why he did that. Maybe the open space is supposed to be a way to welcome his guest.

Jack: And I wonder why almost all of the objects come in pairs. Do you see that? Two chairs, two portraits on the walls, two other framed paintings, two parts to the window, two doors, two pillows, two sets of clothes and towel pegs, two other wall hangings on either side of the windows.

Margaret: Some art historians say that the double effect is Van Gogh's way of saying that he's looking forward to having another person in his house.

Jack: I can see why you like this painting. The more I look at it, the more I can see in it. It also kind of reminds me of my bedroom when I was a kid. It was different, of course, but I always felt safe, warm, and comfortable in it. It was my very own private space.

Margaret: See? And you thought you didn't know much about art!

Activity L: Word connections, p. 90

1. horrific
2. studious
3. serpentine
4. ruinous
5. statuesque
6. shady
7. cruelty
8. accidental
9. picturesque
10. gelatinous

Activity M: Words of the same family, p. 91

Eli: Hey guys. What're you doin' tonight?

Leila: I'm supposed to study for an English exam. It's on Friday, so I don't have much time left. Why do you wanna know?

Eli: Well, I'm thinking of going to the movies tonight. There's an action-adventure movie playing at the State Theater. I don't know who the actors are, but I heard it was pretty exciting. I can't think of the title.

Abe: I think it's called *Train Robbery* or something like that.

Leila: Hm, that doesn't sound very interesting. I think I'd rather study.

Eli: You're kidding, right? Everybody who's seen this movie is crazy about it. Come on. You can't study all the time. There's still tomorrow night.

Abe: Yeah. I'll even buy the popcorn.

Leila: (sighs) Well, I guess I *could* relax one evening. As long as you drive.

Activity S: *True Grit*, p. 96

So, listeners, I saw a great movie over the weekend. *True Grit*, the 2010 version. If you haven't seen it, don't worry. I won't give away the ending. But it's great, and I wanted to share the basics of the story.

The movie is based on a novel written by Charles Portis in 1968. It was so popular that it was made into a film in 1969. John Wayne played the U.S. Marshal and Kim Darby was the main character, Mattie Ross. In 2010, the Coen brothers remade the original movie. In the new version, the cast features Hailee Steinfeld as Mattie Ross, Jeff Bridges as Rooster Cogburn—who's the U.S. Marshal—Josh Brolin as Tom Chaney, and Matt Damon as LaBoeuf. Great cast and superb acting.

So a quick summary. The movie is a western, the setting is Arkansas and the Indian Territory—present-day Oklahoma. And it's set in the mid-nineteenth century. The story is told by Mattie Ross in 1928, when she's an old woman.

The story she tells begins when she was 14 on the Ross family farm. Mattie's father, Frank Ross, hires Tom Chaney to work on the farm. Mattie's a teenage tomboy: intelligent, crafty, and stubborn. And she dislikes Chaney intensely. She calls him "trash" because he's no good at his job. So one day, her father and Tom Chaney ride off to buy some

horses. After they get the horses, they're in a barroom and Chaney gets into a fight with someone. Frank Ross tries to break up the fight; Chaney kills him, steals 150 dollars from him, and escapes into Indian Territory.

This is when Mattie decides that she'll track down the killer and get justice and revenge for the murder of her father. She finds a U.S. Marshal in the district named Reuben J. Cogburn to help her. "Rooster," as he's called, is not a great candidate to help Mattie: he has only one eye, he's overweight, he drinks too much, and he likes to use his gun. But he's really good at looking for outlaws, and Mattie is sure that he has the grit for the job. So she convinces him to hunt down Chaney only if Rooster agrees to let Mattie go with him. As they get ready for the trip, they run into a Texas Ranger named LaBoeuf. He's also following Chaney, and the three of them finally decide to work together.

Their adventures lead them deep into Indian Territory. But along the way, Mattie learns many life lessons, and the two men become very attached to this gutsy girl. She has to cut down a hanged man from a tree, her beloved horse dies, she's taken hostage, she falls into a cavern, and she's bitten by a rattlesnake.

This tale of adventure, friendship, loyalty, and courage was one of the best movies of 2010. I won't tell you how it ends. But I recommend it very highly. Look for it somewhere, watch it with friends, and don't forget the popcorn!

CHAPTER 7

Activity B: What's the problem?, p. 100

1

Celio: And now I just can't pay all the bills. I really don't know how I got myself into this mess.

Barry: Well, it happens. But you've got to figure something out. Could you borrow money from your brother? He seems to be doing pretty well these days.

Celio: I will if I have to, but I'd really rather find another solution.

2

Ramona: This is terrible! How did it happen?

Dennis: I guess I just wasn't watching where I was going. I'll be in a wheelchair for the next *six weeks*!

Ramona: That's really too bad … Guess it just wasn't your day.

3

Will: So what are you going to do about this?

Alicia: Well, I'm going to try to confront my colleague first. But if that doesn't work, I'll have to talk with my manager. That would really be my last resort though.

Will: That's really too bad. I'm so sorry.

4

Leira: So he already had to miss the first game because he had a bad cold. But then, to make matters worse, he comes down with the flu!

Soon-yi: Wow, he just can't catch a break, can he?

Leira: Guess not. At least the coach is understanding.

5

Brock: Hey, what's goin' on with you two?

Freddie: I don't want to go into a lot of detail. It was just a little misunderstanding at first, and then we both said some unkind things.

Brock: Gee, I hope you can work it out.

Freddie: Thanks.

6

Antonio: This is a nightmare! Carlos has soccer practice at 3:00, but I have a doctor's appointment with the baby at 2:30. And then

Anna needs to be picked up at 3:15, but Leanne can't do it because she has a meeting.

Rodrigo: Whoa, take a deep breath. Maybe I can help. I could drop *you* at the doctor, Carlos at soccer, and then pick Anna up on my way back.

Antonio: Really? Oh, you're a lifesaver. I know things'll get better once Anna has her driver's license.

Rodrigo: Ha! You say that *now* …

Activity C: Money troubles, p. 100

(applause)

Sally: Welcome back to the show! We're talking to Brad Burns, the Money Doctor, who's been trying to help solve our money problems. And also here with us is a member of our studio audience, Sean Reese, who would like to talk to Brad about some of his concerns. Welcome Sean.

Sean: Thanks, Sally.

Sally: Now Sean, you say you're in a bit of financial trouble.

Sean: That's right.

Brad: So what's the matter, Sean?

Sean: Well, for starters, I was out of work for about 8 months last year. I found another job, thank goodness, but I've got a real problem on my hands. I have a lot of credit card debt from when I was unemployed.

Brad: That's too bad. Is there any way you can make regular payments on it?

Sean: Well, after making payments on the house and my motorcycle, I barely have enough for gas and food. I'm only making the minimum payment on the credit card bill, and I know that's bad. What am I gonna do?

Brad: Tell me, do you have any other sources of income?

Sean: I'm afraid not. I do have some savings in an "emergency fund," in case I get sick or something, but that's nowhere near enough to pay off the card.

Brad: OK, I think we can figure this out. First, you should hold on to that "emergency money," but the interest you pay on that credit card is going to kill you. You're gonna have to make some changes until you get rid of this debt.

Sean: Like what?

Brad: Well, first, you need more income. You might need to find a second job. If you can work another 15 to 20 hours a week – even at minimum wage – you'll pay off that card much faster.

Sean: I won't have much of a social life, will I?

Brad: Well, no, but that's actually good. You should try not to use your credit card again until it's paid off. In fact, I'd get a plastic bag you can seal, fill it with water, throw that credit card in there, and put the bag in the freezer.

Sally: Freeze the credit card? That's funny.

Brad: Yeah, but it works. And one more thing. You should probably sell your motorcycle and find another way to get to work for awhile. Getting rid of that expense would help a lot.

Sean: My bike? You're probably right. If I make a good plan and stick to it, I guess I could be debt-free in less than a year. But uh … can I think over that motorcycle part a little more?

Activity J: A matter of time, p. 105

1

Rachel: So then, he shows up at my door to pick me up for the camping trip! I had already told him two weeks ago that I couldn't go. So I'm like, "What are you doing here?" He's there at the door while the others are waiting in the car! I couldn't believe it!

Jen: You know, sometimes when you're talking to him, I really don't think he's listening. It wasn't your fault.

2

Frank: … and she was in a real panic. Before I figured out what was going on, I thought it was an emergency and that she needed me to drive her to the hospital. I was so confused.

We laughed about it later, after everything was settled. But this happens to me all the time. When I study, I'm so focused that it's hard for me to come back to reality.

Peter: Gosh, I wish I could concentrate that hard. I'm glad everything's OK, though.

3

Susan: When did this happen?

Alvin: Yesterday morning, at about 9:00. He just backed his car right into mine. I saw him coming before he hit me, but I couldn't move anywhere because I was stopped at a red light. The police came about 15 minutes later and filled out an accident report.

Susan: Did you try honking your horn?

Alvin: Yes! As soon as I saw him coming at me! But he was on his cell phone.

Susan: Well at least no one got hurt.

4

Wife: I just bought those jeans for him two months ago, and now they don't fit.

Husband: Why not?

Wife: Because he grew two inches! I can't keep up.

Husband: He never wore them?

Wife: No, he finally got them out to wear yesterday. That's when I found out.

Husband: Can you return them to the store for a bigger size?

Wife: I already tried that, but they won't take them without a receipt. I think I threw it away when I was cleaning out my purse last week. Do you know how expensive those jeans were?

Husband: I don't want to know.

Activity K: Once upon a knight, p. 106

Once upon a time, Sir Rowan, a knight in the service of King William, returned to the castle, injured. His horse had been stolen the week before when he was attacked and wounded by thieves. Wondering how to get home, he walked for several days before he finally crossed the border into King William's lands. After he entered the castle, the knight was brought to the royal doctor, who bandaged his wounds.

Meanwhile, in another part of the castle, Princess Valaine, the king's daughter, was getting bored with another lecture from her father. The king was telling her again that she needed to settle down and get married. "You are my daughter, but you have the ambition of a knight!" the king complained. At the same moment that the princess was about to tell her father that she actually *wanted* to become a knight, the court minister interrupted with the news of Sir Rowan's arrival. Suddenly the princess no longer felt bored.

While Sir Rowan ate supper, Princess Valaine eagerly asked him questions about his adventures. "Why do you want to know?" asked Sir Rowan. "Being a knight is terrible. I'm tired of fighting!" Then, after hearing the knight's problem, the princess revealed her own problem. For many years, she had been secretly learning the skills to become a knight. But all that time, the king didn't know about the princess's actions, for it was against the rules of the kingdom for women to fight. Even so, for the princess, the king's own daughter, becoming a knight was her dream.

And then the knight had an idea. In those days, the Dragon Grimm terrorized the kingdom, and the king ordered all knights of the realm to track Grimm and destroy him. "If you really want to be a knight," Sir Rowan told Princess Valaine, "take my place in the search for Grimm. I shall tell your father that I will go out alone, find Grimm, and kill him. Then you will disguise yourself in my armor and go. Destroy Grimm, and you will prove yourself worthy to be a knight in your father's service." The princess agreed, but before she left, she asked Sir Rowan what he wanted in return. "To leave the knighthood and become a simple gardener," he replied. And so it was that Sir Rowan hid himself in the castle, while the princess traveled to the land of Grimm.

Three days passed. Then one day, a mysterious figure in armor appeared at the castle door carrying a large sack. As the knight entered the castle, King William was called to the courtyard. "Sir Rowan," said the king, "what say you of your quest?" The knight, in a deep voice, replied, "I have destroyed the Dragon Grimm. In this sack is the monster's heart." As the knight tossed the sack at the king's feet, everyone in the castle cheered. "You have served your kingdom well!" the king exclaimed after the noise died down. "Thank you, … father," and just then the princess removed the helmet from her head. "And now you know I am worthy to be called a knight!" The crowd gasped and the king's eyes grew wide. All was silent. And then the princess bent down on one knee and lowered her head.

The king knew he had no choice. He took her sword and touched her shoulders. "I name you, before these witnesses, a knight of the Court of King William, and …" the king paused, "… my daughter." When the princess stood, the king hugged her.

Activity S: It's a lot to ask … , p. 113

Elena: Excuse me, Mr. Rodriguez, do you have a moment?

Mr. Rodriguez: Of course, Elena. What's up?

Elena: Um … I've got a bit of a problem …

Mr. Rodriguez: OK. Tell me about it.

Elena: Well, my cousin's getting married in Honduras, and I'd really like to be there. The trouble is, the wedding is on a Tuesday, one of the days our class meets.

Mr. Rodriguez: Oh, that's too bad.

Elena: But that's not all. It's on April 23rd, the same day as our final exam.

Mr. Rodriguez: Well, you just can't catch a break!

Elena: I know. I wouldn't even come to you with this if it were just for me. But my mother wants to go too. It's her sister's son who's getting married. But she's older and needs help getting around. So if I don't fly down with her, she probably won't be able to go.

Mr. Rodriguez: So what do you think we should do?

Elena: Well, I know this is a lot to ask, but I'm wondering if there's any way I can take the exam early. Like maybe on the Friday before?

Mr. Rodriguez: Oh, dear. The last week before finals is so crazy. I just don't think I'd be able to write the exam in time for you to take it on that Friday. I'm terribly sorry.

Elena: That's OK. I knew there wasn't much of a chance it would work out. Thanks anyway for considering it.

Mr. Rodriguez: Let me think for a minute. Elena, when does your plane leave?

Elena: First thing in the morning on Monday the 22nd, I'm afraid …

Mr. Rodriguez: OK … How about this? Between Saturday morning and Sunday noon, I should be able to have the test written. If you can come to campus on Sunday afternoon, the reference librarian could give you the exam. She's a friend of mine. I'll e-mail it to her, and you could take it in the library. Would that work for you?

Elena: That would be wonderful. Are you sure that it's not too much trouble though?

Mr. Rodriguez: It should be fine. I have to write it that weekend anyway.

Elena: Oh, this is really, really nice of you. I know how busy you are.

Mr. Rodriguez: I'm just glad we could find a solution.

Elena: Well, I really appreciate your willingness to help me. Have a great weekend, Mr. Rodriguez. See you next week.

Mr. Rodriguez: Bye, Elena.

CHAPTER 8

Activity B: Hypothesis or certainty?, p. 116

1

It would be possible to finish by next Thursday, if it doesn't rain.

2

I'm picking you up at 6:30 so there's no chance we'll be late.

3

If only there were more time! I could do a better job if I just had a couple more days.

4

You know, if I were in your shoes, I'd be a little nicer to her.

5

We'll watch a movie after dinner.

6

You know, if you don't understand this, you could always go and ask your professor for some help.

7

My kid is sick, so I won't be there this afternoon.

8

He's welcome to come with us, but if he backs out again, I am *not* going to pay for his ticket.

9

Thanks for the loan. I'll pay you back as soon as I can.

10

He seems really grouchy today. He must be coming down with a cold.

Activity C: Man's best friend, p. 116

Sister: Hey, what's up?

Brother: Oh, I'm worried about Dad. He just hasn't been himself these past few months. Do you think he might be getting sick or something?

Sister: I doubt it. But let's just say that were true. What could we do about it? You know how much he fights us about going to the doctor.

Brother: Hm. Come to think of it, this started around the time Pepper died. I wonder if we should get him another dog.

Sister: I don't know about that. He and Pepper were like best friends. If we got him another dog, he might think we're trying to replace Pepper.

Brother: We *are* trying to replace Pepper!

Sister: But what if he doesn't like the new dog?

Brother: He loves animals. I imagine he would learn to love a new dog.

Sister: OK, so where would we get it?

Brother: We could check the local animal shelter. They always have a lot of nice dogs there that would love a good home like Dad's. And of course, Dad will have to walk the dog every day. I'll bet he would feel better if he were getting more exercise.

Sister: That's true. What would happen if he goes to Florida this winter? He's been talking about doing that. Who would take care of the dog?

Brother: Well, if that happens, we could take turns feeding it and taking it for walks. I don't know, maybe we're getting ahead of ourselves. This would be an easier decision if we knew he was ready for a new dog. Maybe we should call him.

Activity K: Are you sure?, p. 121

1

If you turn that assignment in late, you're going to get a lower grade.

2

Don't throw that earring away yet. It's possible I *might* still find the other one …

3

Let's imagine for a minute that you *did* win the scholarship.

4

I'm sure he'll be here … He's usually so good at remembering things.

5

If things go the way they have been, notepad computers will weigh less than 8 ounces soon.

6

You could always stay home tonight and try to finish the paper …

7

There's not a chance in the world that he'll keep his promise.

8

I know I can help you.

Activity L: Cultural exchange, p. 122

Journalist: Ms. White, as school principal, you're gaining attention for helping your students learn about world cultures. Please tell us about this.

Ms. White: Well, it's one thing to read about other cultures and quite another to learn about them firsthand. We wondered how we could put our students in contact with students in Africa, Asia, and Europe. We're convinced that with this approach, they will build relationships that make them feel more comfortable with cultural differences.

Journalist: And how are you doing this?

Ms. White: We're using all of the wonderful communication technology we have available today. Our students exchange e-mails, they have video chats, and we've even used Internet conferencing to include our international friends in birthday parties.

Journalist: I'm sure some of these friendships will last a lifetime.

Ms. White: We certainly think so. We're predicting that eventually these friends will want to meet each other in person and make this a true cultural exchange. We wonder what the world would be like if people from different countries started seeing fewer differences.

Journalist: Opportunities like this change people's lives.

Ms. White: I agree. In my opinion, this will remind all of us that there's more to the world than our schools and neighborhoods.

Journalist: That is an important message. I imagine that other schools plan to use your idea.

Ms. White: I just know that schools that try this will never regret it.

Activity U: Uh-oh … , p. 128

Tomas: Hey, Paola, mind if I sit down?

Paola: Sure, maybe you can cheer me up. That class was terrible.

Tomas: No kidding. I bet she's still mad at us. And, I've gotta say, we deserved it. *Nobody* was prepared.

Paola: I would have been prepared if my little brother hadn't been sick. I was the one who had to take care of him. It's always really hard to study when you're worried about something. But then, I suppose *everyone* had an excuse …

Tomas: And every activity she tried to do with us fell flat. I felt awful.

Paola: She was trying to be patient, but when the students aren't prepared, it's hard to do your work. Surely we're going to have a surprise quiz tomorrow. That's her style.

Tomas: You might be right … If we do, I'll be in trouble. I really don't understand that stuff she was explaining today, and I don't know the vocabulary well enough either. Listen, we could study together if you had some time this afternoon or tonight. Maybe we could help each other.

Paola: That would be so great. I know I'll feel better tomorrow if I'm prepared.

Tomas: No problem. People usually learn more when they study with someone. What's that saying? Oh, yeah, "Two heads are better than one."

Paola: *(chuckles):* That's really funny when you think about it. Just imagine if you really had two heads. Anyway, let's meet here at 4:00 if that works for you. If we're not ready tomorrow, it's definitely going to show in our grades!

Speaker's Handbook

1. Greetings, Introductions, and Leave-taking

Greeting someone you know
Hello.
Hi.
Hey.
Morning.
How's it going? *(informal)*
What's up? *(informal)*

Greeting someone you haven't seen for a while
It's good to see you again.
It's been a long time.
How long has it been?
Long time no see! *(informal)*
You look great! *(informal)*
So what have you been up to? *(informal)*

Greeting someone you don't know
Hello.
Good morning.
Good afternoon.
Good evening.
Hi, there! *(informal)*

Saying goodbye
Goodbye.
Bye.
Bye-bye.
See you.
See you later.
Have a good day.
Take care.
Good night. *(only when saying goodbye)*

Introducing yourself
Hi, I'm Tom.
Hello, my name is Tom.
Excuse me.
We haven't met.
My name is Tom. *(formal)*

I saw you in (science) class.
I met you at Jane's party.

Introducing other people
Have you two met?
Have you met Maria?
I'd like you to meet Maria.
There's someone I'd like you to meet.
Let me introduce you to Maria.
> **You:** This is my friend Maria.
> **Ali:** Glad to meet you, Maria.
> **You:** Maria, this is Ali.
> **Maria:** Nice to meet you, Ali.
I've been wanting to meet you.
Tom has told me a lot about you.

Greeting guests
Welcome.
Oh, hi.
How are you?
Please come in.
Glad you could make it.
Did you have any trouble finding us?
Can I take your coat?
Have a seat.
Please make yourself at home.
> **You:** Can I get you something to drink?
> **Guest:** Yes, please.
> **You:** What would you like?
> **Guest:** I'll have some orange juice.
What can I get you to drink?
Would you like some . . . ?

Saying goodbye to guests
Thanks for coming.
Thanks for joining us.
I'm so glad you could come.
It wouldn't have been the same
  without you.
Let me get your things.
Stop by anytime.

2. Having a Conversation

Starting a conversation
Nice weather, huh?
Aren't you a friend of Jim's?
Did you see last night's game?
What's your favorite TV show?
So, what do you think about (the situation in Europe)?
So, how do you like (your new car)?
Guess what I did last night?

Showing that you are listening
Uh-huh.
Right.
Exactly.
Yeah.
OK . . .
I know what you mean.

Giving yourself time to think
Well . . .
Um . . .
Uh . . .
Let me think.
Just a minute.

> **Other:** We should ride our bikes.
> **You:** It's too far. And, I mean . . . , it's raining and we're already late.

Checking for comprehension
Do you see what I mean?
Are you with me?
Does that make sense?

Checking for agreement
Don't you agree?
So what do you think?
We have to (act fast), you know?

Expressing agreement
You're right.
I couldn't agree with you more.
Good thinking! (informal)
You said it! (informal)
You're absolutely right.
Absolutely! (informal)

Expressing disagreement
I'm afraid I disagree.
Yeah, but . . .
I see your point, but . . .
That's not true.

You must be joking! (informal)
No way! (informal)

Asking someone to repeat something
Excuse me?
Sorry?
I didn't quite get that.
Could you repeat that?
Could you say that again?
Say again? (informal)

Interrupting someone
Excuse me.
Yes, but (we don't have enough time).
I know, but (that will take hours).
Wait a minute. (informal)
Just hold it right there! (impolite)

Changing the topic
By the way, what do you think about (the new teacher)?
Before I forget, (there's a free concert on Friday night).
Whatever . . . (Did you see David's new car?)
Enough about me. Let's talk about you.

Ending a conversation
It was nice talking with you.
Good seeing you.
Sorry, I have to go now.

3. Using the Telephone

Making personal calls
Hi, this is David.
Is this Alice?
Is Alice there?
May I speak with Alice, please? (formal)
I work with her.
We're in the same science class.
Could you tell her I called?
Would you ask her to call me?

Answering personal calls
Hello?
Who's calling, please?
Oh, hi, David. How are you?
I can't hear you.
Sorry, we got cut off.
I'm in the middle of something.
Can I call you back?
What's your number again?
Listen. I have to go now.
It was nice talking to you.

Answering machine greetings

You've reached 212-555-6701.

Please leave a message after the beep.

Hi, this is Carlos.

I can't take your call right now.

Sorry I missed your call.

Please leave your name and number.

I'll call you back as soon as I can.

Answering machine messages

This is Magda. Call me back when you
get a chance. *(informal)*

Call me back on my cell.

I'll call you back later.

Talk to you later.

If you get this message before 11:00, please
call me back.

Making business calls

Hello. This is Andy Larson.

I'm calling about . . .

Is this an OK time?

Answering business calls

Apex Electronics. Rosa Baker speaking. *(formal)*

Hello, Rosa Baker.

May I help you?

Who's calling, please?

> **Caller:** May I speak with Mr. Hafner, please?
> **Businessperson:** This is he.

> **Caller:** Mr. Hafner, please.
> **Businessperson:** Speaking.

Talking to an office assistant

Extension 716, please.

Customer Service, please.

May I speak with Sheila Spink, please?

She's expecting my call.

I'm returning her call.

I'd like to leave a message for Ms. Spink.

Making appointments on the phone

> **You:** I'd like to make an appointment to see Ms. Spink.
> **Assistant:** How's 11:00 on Wednesday?
> **You:** Wednesday is really bad for me.
> **Assistant:** Can you make it Thursday at 9:00?
> **You:** That would be perfect!
> **Assistant:** OK. I have you down for Thursday at 9:00.

Special explanations

I'm sorry. She's not available.

Is there something I can help you with?

Can I put you on hold?

I'll transfer you to that extension.

If you leave your number, I'll have Ms. Spink call
you back.

I'll tell her you called.

4. Interviewing for a Job

Small talk by the interviewer

Thanks for coming in today.

Did you have any trouble finding us?

How was the drive?

Would you like a cup of coffee?

Do you happen to know (Terry Mendham)?

Small talk by the candidate

What a great view!

Thanks for arranging to see me.

I've been looking forward to meeting you.

I spent some time exploring the company's website.

My friend, Dale, has worked here for
several years.

Getting serious

OK, shall we get started?

So, anyway . . .

Let's get down to business.

General questions for a candidate

Tell me a little about yourself.

How did you get into this line of work?

How long have you been in this country?

How did you learn about the opening?

What do you know about this company?

Why are you interested in working for us?

General answers to an interviewer

I've always been interested in (finance).

I enjoy (working with numbers).

My (uncle) was (an accountant) and encouraged me to
try it.

I saw your ad in the paper.

This company has a great reputation in the field.

Job-related questions for a candidate

What are your qualifications for this job?
Describe your work experience.
What were your responsibilities on your last job?
I'd like to hear more about (your supervisory experience).

> **Interviewer:** Have you taken any courses in (bookkeeping)?
> **You:** Yes, I took two courses in business school and another online course last year.

What interests you about this particular job?
Why do you think it's a good fit?
Why did you leave your last job?
Do you have any experience with (HTML)?
Would you be willing to (travel eight weeks a year)?
What sort of salary are you looking for?

Describing job qualifications to an interviewer

In (2000), I started working for (Booker's) as a (sales rep).
After (two years), I was promoted to (sales manager).
You'll notice on my resume that (I supervised six people).
I was responsible for (three territories).
I was in charge of (planning sales meetings).
I have experience in all areas of (sales).
I helped implement (online sales reports).
I had to (contact my reps) on a daily basis.
I speak (Spanish) fluently.
I think my strong points are (organization and punctuality).

Ending the interview

I'm impressed with your experience.
I'd like to arrange a second interview.
When would you be able to start?
You'll hear from us by (next Wednesday).
We'll be in touch.

5. Agreeing and Disagreeing

Agreeing

Yeah, that's right.
I know it.
I agree with you.
You're right.
That's true.

I think so, too.
That's what I think.
Me, too.
Me neither.

Agreeing strongly

You're absolutely right!
Definitely!
Certainly!
Exactly!
Absolutely!
Of course!
I couldn't agree more.
You're telling me! *(informal)*
You said it! *(informal)*

Agreeing weakly

I suppose so.
Yeah, I guess so.
It would seem that way.

Remaining neutral

I see your point.
You have a point there.
I understand what you're saying.
I see what you mean.
I'd have to think about that.
I've never thought about it that way before.
Maybe yes, maybe no.
Could be.

Disagreeing

No, I don't think so.
I agree up to a point.
I really don't see it that way.
That's not what I think.
I agree that (going by car is faster), but . . .
But what about (the expense involved)?
Yes, but . . .
I know, but . . .
No, it wasn't. / No, they don't. / *etc.*

> **Other person:** We could save a lot of money by taking the bus.
> **You:** Not really. It would cost almost the same as driving.

Disagreeing strongly

I disagree completely.
That's not true.
That is not an option.
Definitely not!
Absolutely not!
You've made your point, but . . .
No way! *(informal)*
You can't be serious. *(informal)*
You've got to be kidding! *(informal)*
Where did you get that idea? *(impolite)*
Are you out of your mind! *(impolite)*

Disagreeing politely

I'm afraid I have to disagree with you.
I'm not so sure.
I'm not sure that's such a good idea.
I see what you're saying, but . . .
I'm sure many people feel that way, but . . .
But don't you think we should consider (other alternatives)?

6. Interrupting, Clarifying, Checking for Understanding

Informal interruptions

Um.
Sir? / Ma'am?
Just a minute.
Can I stop you for a minute?
Wait a minute! *(impolite)*
Hold it right there! *(impolite)*

Formal interruptions

Excuse me, sir / ma'am.
Excuse me for interrupting.
Forgive me for interrupting you, but . . .
I'm sorry to break in like this, but . . .
Could I interrupt you for a minute?
Could I ask a question, please?

Asking for clarification—Informal

What did you say?
I didn't catch that.
Sorry, I didn't get that.
I missed that.
Could you repeat that?
Could you say that again?

Say again?
I'm lost.
Could you run that by me one more time?
Did you say . . . ?
Do you mean . . . ?

Asking for clarification—Formal

I beg your pardon?
I'm not sure I understand what you're saying.
I can't make sense of what you just said.
Could you explain that in different words?
Could you please repeat that?
Could you go over that again?

Giving clarification—Informal

I'll go over it again.
I'll take it step-by-step.
I'll take a different tack this time.
Stop me if you get lost.
OK, here's a recap.
Maybe this will clarify things.
To put it another way, . . .
In other words, . . .

Giving clarification—Formal

Let me put it another way.
Let me give you some examples.
Here are the main points again.
I'm afraid you didn't understand what I said.
I'm afraid you've missed the point.
What I meant was . . .
I hope you didn't think that . . .
I didn't mean to imply that . . .
I hope that clears things up.

Checking for understanding

Do you understand now?
Is it clearer now?
Do you see what I'm getting at?
Does that help?
Is there anything that still isn't clear?
What other questions do you have?
  Speaker: What else?
  Listener: I'm still not clear on the difference between a preposition and a conjunction.
Now explain it to me in your own words.

7. Apologizing

Apologizing for a small accident or mistake

Sorry.

I'm sorry.

Excuse me.

It was an accident.

Pardon me. (formal)

Oops! (informal)

My mistake. (informal)

I'm terrible with (names).

I've never been good with (numbers).

I can't believe I (did) that.

Apologizing for a serious accident or mistake

I'm so sorry.

I am really sorry that I (damaged your car).

I am so sorry about (damaging your car).

I feel terrible about (the accident).

I'm really sorry, but (I was being very careful).

I'm sorry for (causing you a problem).

Please accept my apologies for . . . (formal)

I sincerely apologize for . . . (formal)

Apologizing for upsetting someone

I'm sorry I upset you.

I didn't mean to make you feel bad.

Please forgive me. (formal)

I just wasn't thinking straight.

That's not what I meant to say.

I didn't mean it personally.

I'm sorry. I'm having a rough day.

Apologizing for having to say no

I'm sorry. I can't.

Sorry, I never (lend anyone my car).

I wish I could say yes.

I'm going to have to say no.

I can't. I have to (work that evening).

Maybe some other time.

Responding to an apology

Don't worry about it.

Oh, that's OK.

Think nothing of it. (formal)

Don't mention it. (formal)

> **Other person:** I'm afraid I lost the pen you lent me.
> **You:** No big thing.

It doesn't matter.

It's not important.

Never mind.

No problem.

It happens.

Forget it.

Don't sweat it. (informal)

Apology accepted. (formal)

Showing regret

I feel really bad.

It won't happen again.

I wish I could go back and start all over again.

I don't know what came over me.

I don't know what to say.

Now I know better.

Too bad I didn't . . .

It was inexcusable of me. (formal)

It's not like me to . . .

I hope I can make it up to you.

That didn't come out right.

I didn't mean to take it out on you.

Sympathizing

This must be very difficult for you.

I know what you mean.

I know how you're feeling.

I know how upset you must be.

I can imagine how difficult this is for you.

8. Suggestions, Advice, Insistence

Making informal suggestions

Here's what I suggest.

I know what you should do.

Why don't you (go to the movies with Jane)?

What about (having lunch with Bob)?

Try (the French fries next time).

Have you thought about (riding your bike to work)?

Accepting suggestions

Thanks, I'll do that.

Good idea!

That's a great idea.

Sounds good to me.

That's a plan.

I'll give it a try.

Guess it's worth a try.

Refusing suggestions

No. I don't like (French fries).

That's not for me.

I don't think so.

That might work for some people, but . . .

Nawww. (informal)

I don't feel like it. (impolite)

Giving serious advice—Informal

Listen!

Here's the plan.

Take my advice.

Take it from one who knows.

Take it from someone who's been there.

Here's what I think you should do.

Hey! Here's an idea.

How about (waiting until you're 30 to get married)?

Don't (settle down too quickly).

Why don't you (see the world while you're young)?

You can always (settle down later).

Don't forget—(you only live once).

Giving serious advice—Formal

Have you ever thought about (becoming a doctor)?

Maybe it would be a good idea if you (went back to school).

It looks to me like (Harvard) would be your best choice.

If I were you, I'd (study medicine).

In my opinion, you should (consider it seriously).

Be sure to (get your application in early).

I always advise people to (check that it was received).

The best idea is (to study hard).

If you're really smart, you'll (start right away).

Accepting advice

You're right.

Thanks for the advice.

That makes a lot of sense.

I see what you mean.

That sounds like good advice.

I'll give it a try.

I'll do my best.

You've given me something to think about.

I'll try it and get back to you.

Refusing advice

I don't think that would work for me.

That doesn't make sense to me.

I'm not sure that would be such a good idea.

I could never (become a doctor).

Thanks for the input.

Thanks, but no thanks. (informal)

You don't know what you're talking about. (impolite)

I think I know what's best for myself. (impolite)

Back off! (impolite)

Insisting

You have to (become a doctor).

Try to see it my way.

I know what I'm talking about.

If you don't (go to medical school), I won't (pay for your college).

I don't care what you think. (impolite)

9. Describing Feelings

Happiness

I'm doing great.

This is the best day of my life.

I've never been so happy in my life.

I'm so pleased for you.

Aren't you thrilled?

What could be better?

Life is good.

Sadness

Are you OK?

Why the long face?

I'm not doing so well.

I feel awful.

I'm devastated.

I'm depressed.

I'm feeling kind of blue.

I just want to crawl in a hole.

Oh, what's the use?

Fear

I'm worried about (money).

He dreads (going to the dentist).

I'm afraid to (drive over bridges).

She can't stand (snakes).

This anxiety is killing me.

He's scared of (big dogs).

How will I ever (pass Friday's test)?

I have a phobia about (germs).

Anger

I'm really mad at (you).
They resent (such high taxes).
How could she (do) that?
I'm annoyed with (the neighbors).
(The noise of car alarms) infuriates her.
He was furious with (the children).

Boredom

I'm so bored.
There's nothing to do around here.
What a bore!
Nothing ever happens.
She was bored to tears.
They were bored to death.
I was bored stiff.
It was such a monotonous (movie).
(That TV show) was so dull.

Disgust

That's disgusting.
Eeew! Yuck! *(informal)*
I hate (raw fish).
How can you stand it?
I almost vomited.
I thought I'd puke. *(impolite)*
I don't even like to think about it.
How can you say something like that?
I wouldn't be caught dead (wearing that
    dirty old coat).

Compassion

I'm sorry.
I understand what you're going through.
Tell me about it.
How can I help?
Is there anything I can do?
She is concerned about him.
He worries about (the children).
He cares for her deeply.
My heart goes out to them. *(old-fashioned)*

Guilt

I feel terrible that I (lost your mother's necklace).
I never should have (borrowed it).
I feel so guilty!
It's all my fault.
I blame myself.
I make a mess of everything.
I'll never forgive myself.

Photo Credits

Preliminary Chapter

Page x: Neil Marriot/Digital Vision **Page 2:** Duncan de young/berean/iStockphoto.com **Page 3:** top right frender; top left age footstock/Superstock; center right komargallery center left Jodi Matthews/iStockphoto.com **Page 5:** Purestock/Jupiter Images **Page 7:** Deborah Cheramie **Page 8:** Laure Neish/iStockphoto.com

Chapter 1

Page 12: Mojca Odar/Shutterstock **Page 13:** top right Bill Bachmann/Alamy; center right theirry Maffeis/iStockphoto.com; bottom right Andyworks/iStockphoto.com **Page 14:** Sreedhar Yedlapati/iStockphoto.com **Page 16:** top center Jan Paul Schrage; center Nikada/iStockphoto.com; center 4FR/iStockphoto.com; bottom center Eduardo Leite/iStockphoto.com **Page 18:** center right Janine Lamontagne/iStockphoto.com; bottom right fumumpa/iStockphoto.com **Page 19:** top center Kenneth Wiedemann; top right Daniel Deitschel/iStockphoto.com; bottom left Paul Flemming/iStockphoto.com; center right Terraxplorer/iStockphoto.com **Page 20:** Morozova Oxana/Shutterstock **Page 21:** center left Wendy Olsen/iStockphoto.com; center right Maria Grushevskaya/iStockphoto.com **Page 24:** center left Giraudon/The Bridgeman Art Library; center right Private Collection/The Bridgeman Art Library; bottom left National Trust Photographic Library/Derrick E. Witty/The Bridgeman Art Library; bottom right Francis G. Mayer/CORBIS **Page 25:** top center Nikada/iStockphoto.com

Chapter 2

Page 28: Bob Pardue - Lifestyle/Alamy **Page 29:** top left Yuriy Chaban/iStockphoto.com; top right Billy E. Barnes/PhotoEdit **Page 31:** center left Ira Block/National Geographic/Getty Images; center left Alexey Gorbatenkov/iStockphoto.com; center David McShane/iStockphoto.com; center right Kristen Johansen; bottom left james boulette/iStockphoto; bottom center Rick Rhay/iStockphoto.com **Page 33:** Creatas Images/Jupiter Images

Chapter 3

Page 38: Blend_Images/iStockphoto **Page 40:** top right Carlos Oliveras/iStockphoto **Page 42:** top left Elisanth/Shutterstock; top right M. Unal Ozmen/Shutterstock; center left ER_09/Shutterstock; center right Venus Angel/Shutterstock; bottom left artkamalov/Shutterstock; bottom right Mi.Ti/Shutterstock **Page 43:** top center shutswis/Shutterstock; top center zhangyang13576997233/Shutterstock; center Ilona Baha/Shutterstock; bottom center vichie81/Shutterstock; bottom center Lev Kropotov/Shutterstock **Page 44:** top center Chachoo/Shutterstock; center left Ljupco Smokovski/Shutterstock; center right Nicholas

Piccillo/Shutterstock; bottom left aliensprog/Shutterstock; bottom right 3dimentii/Shutterstock.com **Page 50:** Kurt Gordon/istockphoto.com **Page 51:** top right Sandra Kemppainen/Shutterstock.com; bottom left ilker canikligil/Shutterstock.com; bottom center Oleksiy Mark/scanrail/iStockphoto; center left Ljiljana Pavkov/shishic/iStockphoto; center grocap/Shutterstock.com; center right John Kasawa/Shutterstock.com; bottom right malerapaso/iStockphoto **Page 52:** center right Julija Sapic/simplytheyu/iStockphoto; bottom left Mike Flippo/Shutterstock.com; bottom center Gregory Gerber/Shutterstock.com; bottom right David Lee/Shutterstock.com **Page 53:** top left Ivan Stevanovic/istockphoto; top center Komar Maria/Shutterstock; top right Trevor Buttery/Shutterstock; center left Photosindiacom, LLC/Shutterstock; center omers/Shutterstock; center right thefinalmiracle/Shutterstock.com; bottom left ifet/Shutterstock; bottom center discpicture/Shutterstock; bottom right qushe/Shutterstock

Chapter 4

Page 54: © Jacob Wackerhausen/iStockphoto.com **Page 55:** Jim Jurica/tacojim/iStockphoto.com **Page 56:** top left Kirby Hamilton/iStockphoto.com; center left Lilli Day/iStockphoto.com; bottom left Don Bayley/RapidEye/iStockphoto.com **Page 57:** top right Alex Newcombe /Alamy; top center ACE STOCK LIMITED/Alamy **Page 58:** zorani/iStockphoto.com **Page 59:** jocic/Shutterstock **Page 60:** paolo airenti/Shutterstock **Page 61:** top right Suprijono Suharjoto/iStockphoto.com; bottom center Blaj Gabriel/Shutterstock **Page 64:** Erik De Castro, Pool/AP Photos **Page 66:** CSU Archives/Everett Collection **Page 67:** top center SimonKr d.o.o./iStockphoto.com; bottom center Seamartini / Alamy

Chapter 5

Page 68: Daniel Deitschel/iStockphoto.com **Page 69:** Catherine Lane/iStockphoto.com **Page 70:** paparazzit/Shutterstock.com **Page 72:** Sean Locke **Page 75:** Lise Gagne/iStockphoto.com **Page 77:** Radin Myroslav/Shutterstock **Page 78:** Don Bayley/iStockphoto.com **Page 79:** Diane Diederich/iStockphoto.com **Page 80:** René Mansi/iStockphoto.com **Page 81:** Cynthia Farmer/Shutterstock

Chapter 6

Page 83: bottom right Tattoo by Scott Harrison, courtesy of David Bragger **Page 91:** bottom left Michael Nicholson/Corbis; bottom right Deklofenak/Shutterstock **Page 92:** top right Lorey Sebastian/handout/dpa/Corbis **Page 96:** top right Everett Collection; bottom center Prendergast, Maurice Brazil/The Bridgeman Art Library **Page 97:** top left Gogh, Vincent van (1853-90)/The Bridgeman Art Library; top right Shkol'nik, Iosif Solomonovich/The Bridgeman Art Library

Chapter 7

Page 98: Agata Malchrowicz/iStockphoto.com **Page 99**: Sean Locke/iStockphoto.com **Page 100:** top left Brad Killer/iStockphoto.com; top right Rudyanto Wijaya/iStockphoto.com; top left Malte Roger/iStockphoto.com; center left Tetra Images/Alamy; top right berekin/iStockphoto.com; center right RTimages/Shutterstock **Page 101:** Don Bayley/iStockphoto.com **Page 104:** Alashi/iStockphoto.com **Page 106:** fotofrankyat/iStockphoto.com **Page 108:** Jorgen Jacobsen/iStockphoto.com **Page 110:** top right Fancy/Alamy; top center aletermi/Shutterstock; center rawcaptured/Shutterstock; center Dennis MacDonald/Alamy; bottom center Tamara Lackey/fStop/Alamy; **Page 111:** top center Vitaly Titov/iStockphoto.com; bottom right allesalltag/Alamy **Page 112:** Pali Rao/iStockphoto.com **Page 113:** Robert Rushton/iStockphoto.com

Chapter 8

Page 114: drbimages/iStockphoto.com **Page 116:** Europe-Spain/Alamy **Page 117:** Neil Sorenson/iStockphoto.com **Page 119:** Pamela Moore/iStockphoto.com **Page 120:** bottom center imagebroker/Alamy; center right kristian sekulic **Page 123:** Chad McDermott/iStockphoto.com **Page 124:** top right Alan Poulson/iStockphoto.com; top center Ian Shaw/Alamy; center Scho/Relaximages/Alamy; bottom center Patrick Bennett / Alamy; center right AsiaPix/Asia Images Group Pte Ltd/Alamy; bottom right Pictorial Press Ltd/Alamy **Page 126:** Pgiam/iStockphoto.com **Page 127:** narvikk/iStockphoto.com **Page 128:** VikramRaghuvanshi/iStockphoto.com **Page 129:** center Dr_Flash,2009/ Used under license from Shutterstock.com; bottom left Laurin Rinder/Shutterstock; bottom right Jetrel/Shutterstock